# ENGLISH Direct 2

John Foster
Keith West

## Collins Educational
*An imprint of* HarperCollins*Publisher*

Published by Collins Educational

An imprint of HarperCollins*Publishers* Ltd
77–85 Fulham Palace Road
London W6 8JB

© HarperCollins*Publishers* Ltd 1998

First published 1998
**Reprinted 1998**

ISBN 000 323 068 6

John Foster and Keith West assert the moral right to be identified as the authors of this work.

British Library Cataloguing in Publication Data. A catalogue record for this book is available from the British Library.

Commissioned by Domenica de Rosa

Edited by Kim Richardson and Lisa English

Picture research by Katie Anderson and Caroline Thompson

Production by Susan Cashin

Design and layout by Ken Vail Graphic Design, Cambridge

Cover design by Ken Vail Graphic Design, Cambridge

Cover photographs: Getty Images and Telegraph Colour Library

Printed and bound by Printing Express Ltd, Hong Kong

### Acknowledgements
The following permissions to reproduce material are gratefully acknowledged. Numbers refer to pages.

#### Illustrations
John Walmsley (6 both, 12, 16 top left, 50 centre, 59, 60 top, 61, 62, 64, 85, 88); Sylvia Poggio Artists Agency (Sean Victory) (7, 13, 16 centre & bottom, 39, 86); Still Pictures/Mark Edwards (8 left); J. Allan Cash Ltd (8 right, 32 top); Clinton Banbury (11, 19, 49, 69, 71, 73, 74, 75); © Katie Vandyck 1993 (14); Reed Books (15); Frances Jordan (18, 27, 43, 48, 92, 93); Getty Images (20 centre, 22 both); Judy Brown (23, 35, 41, 55, 63, 68, 76); Angus Mill (24, 28, 37, 50 top left, 51); Redferns/Des Willie (25); Redferns/Nicky J. Sims (26); Sarah Geeves (29, 30, 42, 77, 82, 83); Harry Venning (31, 44, 53, 65); Telegraph Colour Library (32 left); Heinz logo appears courtesy of H. J. Heinz Ltd (32); Oakwood Leisure Ltd (33); Leisure Sport Ltd/Thorpe Park (34); Boots the Chemist (36); The Advertising Archives (38 both); D. C. Thompson and Co Ltd (51, 52); All Sport/Gary M. Prior (56); Redferns/Corey Brandon (57 both); Network/G. Mendal (60 centre); John Birdsall Photography (60 bottom); Caroline Thompson (67); NASA (70 top left); Fortean Picture Library (70 centre); Alan Marks (78, 79, 89, 91).

*Text extracts*
Interview with Jamila Gavin, © Jamila Gavin (14–15); 'Badminton' and 'Ice Hockey' are adapted from entries in *The Oxford Children's Encyclopedia*, published by Oxford University Press (22); Review of OTT is from *Shout Magazine* issue 104, published by D. C. Thompson and Co Ltd (26); Book reviews in 'Family Fortunes' are from *The Young Telegraph*, 22 March 1997 (28); The information on Oakwood is adapted courtesy of Oakwood Leisure Ltd (33); The information on Thorpe Park is adapted courtesy of Leisure Sport Ltd (34); 'Useless' by Paul Higgins is from *The Poetry Processor Book 2* by Paul Higgins, published by Stanley Thornes (Publishers) Ltd (48); 'The Fright of My Life' is from *Shout Magazine* issue 96, published by D. C. Thompson and Co Ltd (52); Penny's story is taken from the article 'Holiday Horrors', published in *Shout Magazine* issue 91 (53); Claire Jeffrey's and Harriet Slack's letters are from *The Young Telegraph*, 19 April 1997 (64); The acting activity on *The Pardoner's Tale* is based on an activity in *New Perspectives 1* by Angela Bell and Hugh Knight, published by Oxford University Press (79); The map and text 'The origins of the English language' are adapted from *Knowledge About Language* by Kevin Burrell, published by Thomas Nelson (81); 'How Ganesh Became Rich and Famous' is adapted from the story 'The Man of Many Mistakes' in *Worlds of English and Drama* by Giles Bird and Jay Norris, published by Oxford University Press (82–83); 'Joshua' by James Rigg – James Rigg is a pseudonym for John Foster and Keith West (86); 'Rule Four: Keep Clear of Pringle' is an extract from *Homebird* by Terence Blacker, published by HarperCollins*Publishers* (88–89); 'Mixed Doubles' is by David Williams (94–95).

Whilst every effort has been made to contact the copyright-holders, this has not proved possible in every case.

# Contents

# English Direct – Complete Coverage of the National Curriculum

| English Direct 1 Year 7 | English Direct 2 Year 8 | English Direct 3 Year 9 |
|---|---|---|
| **Personal Writing** *Topic* Autobiography *Language focus* Drafting | **Personal Writing 6** *Topics* A class who's who; My life; Letter to a penfriend *Language focus* Capital letters and full stops; Letter writing; Verbs and tenses | **Personal Writing** *Topic* Diaries *Language focus* Spelling |
| **Conveying Information** *Topics* Messages and instructions; School rules; Class outings *Language focus* Letter writing; IT skills | **Conveying Information 16** *Topics* My hobby; Animal fact files; An A–Z of sports *Language focus* Drafting and delivering a talk | **Conveying Information** *Topics* Factsheets; Leaflets *Language focus* Sentences |
| **Expressing Opinions** *Topics* TV programmes; Films and videos *Language focus* Sentences; Capital letters | **Expressing Opinions 24** *Topics* Pop shows; CDs; Book reviews *Language focus* Spelling | **Expressing Opinions** *Topics* Computer games *Language focus* Paragraphs |
| **Persuading** *Topics* Safety leaflets; Cautionary tales *Language focus* Spelling | **Persuading 32** *Topic* Advertising *Language focus* Adjectives; Spelling | **Persuading** *Topics* Brochures and leaflets *Language focus* Punctuation |
| **Poetry** *Topics* Shape poems; List poems; Recipe poems; Limericks; Performance poems *Language focus* Nouns; Verbs | **Poetry 42** *Topic* Comparison poems *Language focus* Similes; Drafting | **Poetry** *Topic* Ballads and raps *Language focus* Accent and dialect |
| **Media Texts** *Topics* Comics; Graphic novels *Language focus* Exclamation marks; Spelling | **Media Texts 50** *Topic* Magazines *Language focus* IT skills | **Media Texts** *Topic* Newspapers *Language focus* IT skills |
| **Developing Arguments** *Topic* Letters to newspapers *Language focus* Drafting; Punctuation | **Developing Arguments 60** *Topics* Heroes; The school I'd like; Letters to newspapers *Language focus* Paragraphs; Conjunctions; Commas | **Developing Arguments** *Topics* How adults treat teenagers *Language focus* Drafting and delivering speeches |
| **Storytelling** *Topic* Ghost stories *Language focus* Paragraphs; Plots | **Storytelling 70** *Topics* UFOs; Science-fiction stories *Language focus* Punctuation | **Storytelling** *Topic* Describing characters *Language focus* Drafting |
| **Stories from the Past** *Topics* Myths and legends *Language focus* Library skills; Dictionary skills | **Stories from the Past 78** *Topics* The Canterbury Tales; An Indian folk tale; An American story and poem *Language focus* The development of the English language; Dictionary skills | **Stories from the Past** *Topics* Shakespeare's *Macbeth* *Language focus* The development of the English language |
| **Scripts and Scriptwriting** *Topics* Playscripts; Radio scripts *Language focus* Accents and dialects | **Scripts and Scriptwriting 88** *Topic* Writing and performing scripts *Language focus* Accent and dialect | **Scripts and Scriptwriting** *Topic* From script to screen *Language focus* Register |

**The units** Each unit looks at a particular way in which language is used. For example, in the first unit ('Personal Writing') you will be looking at how language is used to write personal profiles of your classmates. You will then have an opportunity to write about yourself and your family in the form of a letter to a penfriend. Finally, you will see how a famous author writes about herself and her experiences.

Each unit is divided into short chapters, which deal with different topics. For example, the first chapter in the book is called 'A Class Who's Who'.

The chapters also contain several different kinds of activity, which will help you to develop your basic skills in English. The boxes on the rest of this page tell you more about these activities, and give you some advice about how to do them.

# To the Student

## Speaking and Listening

There are a variety of speaking and listening activities, including story-telling, role-plays and making tape-recordings, as well as discussions. These will help you to develop your ability to speak confidently in various situations.

- Take turns to speak.
- Remember to listen carefully when others are speaking.
- When it is your turn, make sure you speak clearly.

## Writing

The writing activities will help you to learn how to express yourself well. You will be trying different kinds of writing, such as fact files, poems and advertisements. You will also have the chance to design leaflets, storyboards and magazines.

- Think about the question or topic before you start writing.
- If you are answering questions on a passage in the book, look back over the passage carefully before you write.
- When you have finished, re-read what you have written, and correct any mistakes.

## Reading

You will be reading all kinds of material, such as short stories, play scripts, poems and letters. The reading activities will help you to develop your ability to read with understanding.

- Read the passages slowly and carefully.
- If you don't understand any words, don't give up: they may become clear later. (Or you can ask your teacher for help.)
- Look at the pictures: they may help you understand what is going on.

## Other activities

- Several activities in this book will help you to improve your grammar, punctuation and spelling.
- Some units have activities that will help you find your way around a dictionary, and practise using a word processor and desk-top publishing programs.
- Other activities include giving a talk to the class, planning a TV show and performing a scene from a play.

is to be a TV ope

# This Is My Life

## I Live in Nigeria ...

**My name is Maria** and I'm thirteen years old. I live with my family in a small village called Alariasa in southern Nigeria. Alariasa is 30 kilometres from the nearest town.

Alariasa is surrounded by farmland and thick forest. We live on the edge of the village, so we can walk out of the house straight into the fields. My father is a farmer. He grows green vegetables, maize and yams on the farm. Yams are like huge potatoes. We mash them into a delicious meal called 'iyan'.

### Helping out

Sometimes, in the school holidays, I help my father and brothers on the farm. There's always a lot of weeds to clear, and everything has to be done by hand. Usually, though, I help my mother, Adeola. As well as looking after my two baby sisters, she has to collect water from the river, which is twenty minutes' walk away, and gather firewood from the forest.

Most men in the village have two wives. My father's second wife is called Sade. She's brilliant at making pots, and she is teaching me how to do it. Some of them are huge – these are for storing water and cooking yams. We make the pots out of clay and bake them in a fire behind the house. Sade is full of songs and laughter – I love working with her.

### Markets and festivals

Every Friday there is a market in the village. My mother and Sade go there if we have any vegetables or pots to sell, and to meet other women from the village. I go there with them if I can, because it is always a colourful and lively occasion – noisy, too, with all the birds and live animals for sale.

We are Yoruba people, and we speak the Yoruba language. My parents and my eldest brother still follow the Yoruba religion, although the rest of my family, including me, are Christians. I still enjoy the Yoruba festivals, though. All the Yoruba gods have their own festivals, where there is a lot of music and dancing and prayers. The priests often wear large wooden masks carved by men in the village.

### At school

I go to St Patrick's Roman Catholic School with three of my brothers and sisters. The school is in the next village, so we have to get up early to walk there. I learn English, Yoruba, Maths and many other subjects, but my favourite subjects are Art and Bible Studies.

I enjoy school, but nothing can beat playing and working at home!

# Reading and Writing

1 Read the article about Maria (page 8). Then work with a partner and write down ten pieces of information that it tells you about Maria and what life is like in Nigeria.

2 Make a list of ten pieces of information that you would put in a similar article about yourself. You could include information about:
- your family
- your home
- your pets
- your school
- your hobbies
- your holidays.

3 Plan and draft an article 'I live in ...', telling magazine readers in another country about your life. If you can, find some photographs of yourself and make a page about yourself like the article 'I Live in Nigeria'.

# Capital Letters and Full Stops

Remember to write proper sentences, starting each one with a capital letter and ending each one with a full stop.

Remember to use capital letters:

- for the first letter of a person's name, for example, Anil Mankad;
- for the first letter of the name of a place, for example, Bradford.

Below is what Alexandra wrote in her article about her school. Copy it out and correct it by putting in capital letters and full stops.

i go to westbourne park school it's a big comprehensive school for boys and girls i am in year 8 and my brother trevor is in year 10 my favourite subjects are science and art i'm learning french but i'm not very good at it we travel to school on a double-decker bus because westbourne is five miles from our house

# Letters to a Penfriend

## Speaking and Listening

In pairs, discuss all the information you would want a new penfriend to tell you about themselves in their first letter to you.

## Writing

Study the letters on this page, which give details of some imaginary people who are looking for a penfriend. Choose one of them and write a letter introducing yourself to her or him. Before you begin, study page 11, which reminds you how to lay out a letter and how to use paragraphs.

Hello penfriends out there,

I'm tall and skinny and I like watching programmes like the X Files. There is life on other planets and they do visit us, I'm sure. What do you think?

At home, I have three brothers and two sisters. My dad owns a restaurant. We cook special Indian food and some English, like chips and sausages.

We've got three cats – Ginger, Sockie and Spots. Spots is a kitten, he's very naughty. One day, Spots caught a mouse and took it upstairs. He dropped the mouse on my bed. It was still alive, and I took all day trying to capture it! Sockie has four white paws. She's really old and going blind. She was a kitten before I was born.

At school, I'm in top set for maths and science, but in the third set for English.

Hope you'll write to me,

Cheers, Sunil Gupta

Dear Friend,

I'm a skateboard freak. I go to the local park and join my mates on the skateboard run. We can jump over boards and small ditches. I've got a helmet and knee pads but I've still hurt myself. I've been in hospital twice – once I broke my arm. I've not been put off, I like skateboarding so much.

I also like mending things like motorbikes, clocks and watches. I like to see how things work. If I had the chance, I'd work on a car engine.

I have a second-hand CD player, but I can only afford a few CDs. My favourite groups are Foo Fighters and Silver Chair. I'm into grunge music.

We have a pet dog at home. He's half Alsatian and half Labrador. He's big and black and funny. He ran away once and we had to look for him in the street. He never bites anyone.

Do write,

Adrian Stevens

Hi, please write to me. I'm into the Spice Girls. My bedroom is covered with posters of the girls in concert. 'Posh Spice' is my favourite — my friends say I look a bit like her, only younger.

When I'm older, I want to sing in an all-girl band. I live with my mum and big sister. They think I'm a pain!

I like London. We can hop on the underground and go anywhere.

Mum took us to Devon for our holidays, to stay with my auntie on a farm. It was brilliant.

All the best,

Melissa Brown

# Letter Layout

Make sure you lay your letter out properly.

- Put your address in the top right-hand corner.
- Start the letter 'Dear …' and end it with 'Yours sincerely'.
- Sign your name and write it in capital letters underneath your signature.
- Remember to use paragraphs. A **paragraph** is a group of sentences, all of which are about the same idea and subject.

Sammy laid out his letter properly (below).

Your address

The date

This is how you begin

Paragraph 1
Me and
my family

Paragraph 2
Our house

Paragraph 3
My school

Paragraph 4
My pet

This is how
you end

Sign and print name

64 Northern Avenue
Woolchester W3 0DH
2 September 2000

Dear Serena,

There are five of us in my family – my mum and dad, my two brothers and me. I'm 13 and I'm the youngest. My big brother is 18. He's great. He's just passed his driving test so he sometimes drives me to the disco in town. My other brother, Brian, is 16 and he's always ordering me about. My dad works for the local council as a gardener in their Parks department and my mum works in a bakery.

We live in a semi-detached house. We've just moved in, so we're redecorating it. My bedroom has wallpaper of men in top hats and long coats riding funny bicycles called penny farthings. I want to take it off and paint my room black, but Dad won't let me.

I go to the local comprehensive school. It's called St Jude's. I'm in Year 8 and I'm in Mr Bloor's class. There are 30 of us in our class. My best subjects are Technology and P.E. I'm always getting told off for forgetting my homework.

I've got a pet rat. He's brown and he's called Bruce. One day Bruce got out of his cage and ate his way through my brother's football magazines. He wouldn't speak to me for days. (My brother, not Bruce!)

Please write soon and tell me all about yourself.

Yours sincerely,

Sammy Walters
SAMMY WALTERS

# A Letter to a Friend

18 High Street
Northtown
West Yorkshire
WY16 1NN
21 June 1999

Dear Jyothi,

It's my dad's birthday at the weekend, so we're having a barbecue on Saturday. Mum said I could ask a friend. Will you be able to come?

It will start at about 7.30 p.m. and go on till late. Mum says you can sleep over, if your mum will let you.

I do hope you can come. Please let me know.

Love,

Kim

When you write a short note like this to a friend, you should always lay the letter out properly. But you do not need to end it with 'Yours sincerely'. You can end it in a friendly way, as Kim does.

## Writing

Practise your letter-writing skills.

1 Write Jyothi's reply.

2 Imagine you have been given two free tickets to go to Alton Towers and that your dad has agreed to take you and a friend. Write a letter inviting a friend to go with you.

3 Write a letter asking a friend if they would like to go to the youth club disco with you.

# Present, Past and Future – Verbs and Tenses

**Verbs** are action words.

The verb is a key word in a sentence. It tells you:

- if the action <u>is happening</u> – in the <u>present</u>;
- if the action <u>has happened</u> – in the <u>past</u>;
- if the action <u>will happen</u> – in the <u>future</u>.

Verbs have different forms or **tenses** to tell you whether an action is taking place in the present, in the past or in the future.

**Present tense**
Sandra <u>is diving</u> into the pool.

**Past tense**
Sandra <u>dived</u> into the pool.

**Future tense**
Sandra <u>will dive</u> into the pool again.

# Writing

Copy out these sentences, underline the verb and say if it is in the present, past or future tense. The first one has been done for you.

1 Germany won the World Cup.
*Germany <u>won</u> the World Cup.* (Past tense)

2 My sister has red hair.

3 We will go on the log flume at Alton Towers.

4 Nick was wearing a blue T-shirt.

5 Trevor is making a sandwich for his supper.

6 We took the dog for a walk in the park.

7 I was waiting for you outside the shop.

8 We will be late for the bus.

9 Javed came third in the competition.

10 The shops are closed on Easter Monday.

11 Natasha has finished the jigsaw puzzle.

12 I dream about being famous one day.

# Meet the Author

## Meet the author: Jamila Gavin

Jamila Gavin is the author of many books for children. Here she answers some questions about herself.

### Where were you born?

I was born in the hills at the foot of the Himalayan mountains in northern India, so I am very fond of mountains. My father was Indian and my mother was English. My earliest memories are of travelling by sea between India and England on huge ocean liners, so I have a great love of the sea as well.

### Do you see yourself as Indian or English?

Because I am half Indian and half English, I got used to describing myself as half and half. It is sometimes expected that people like me will be confused or torn between two different cultures. Since I was brought up to value and admire them both, I have never felt like that.

### Do you remember your own childhood?

Yes. My memories are very sharp and I realise how happy I was then.

### How old were you when you came to live in England, and did you like it?

I was nearly twelve when we finally settled here, although I had been on visits when I was younger. As a child, I didn't think about whether I liked it or not. I was a happy sort of person and I made friends easily. But looking back I realise that I found it cold and I wasn't as free as I had been in India.

### Did you like reading when you were a child?

Yes – I was a word addict. I read anything, even the backs of cornflakes packets. I would spend hours in the bathroom just to get some peace to read, or hiding behind the sofa with a pile of comics.

### How did you become a writer?

I have always liked writing and telling stories, even when I was a very young child. But it was only when I had my own children that I started to take a serious interest in children's books. There are now many more children in Britain like mine, who come from mixed backgrounds. I felt that there were not enough books about children like them. So I started to write books about characters who had similar experiences to them.

*Do you think it's important to understand different cultures?*

Yes. Very important. Almost every war and conflict you can think of has been between people of a different religion, race or colour. I believe that if we want a peaceful world we must understand each other and learn to love our differences.

*Do you like being a writer?*

Sometimes. Mostly, it's lonely. It's easy to lose confidence. But just when I begin to despair, something wonderful happens. I get a brilliant idea and it starts to flow. Then the reward is so fantastic that I never want to stop.

*Where do you get your ideas from?*

From anywhere and everywhere. I might hear someone say something or read an article in a newspaper. I might see someone in a school or in a train. They can all trigger a story, but it is impossible not to be influenced by my own experiences.

*Have you any other ambitions?*

Well, apart from abolishing war, I'd like to sail up the Amazon and take part in the Monte Carlo rally before I'm too old.

# Speaking and Listening

1  In pairs, study the information about Jamila Gavin.

2  Make notes, listing what you learn about her under three headings:
   ● her family and childhood
   ● her writing
   ● her views on belonging to different cultures.

3  Then form groups and compare your lists, before sharing what you have learned about her in a class discussion.

# Reading

Read one of Jamila Gavin's books, then give a short talk to the class. Tell them what the story was about and say why you enjoyed or did not enjoy the book.

In this unit you will be talking and writing in order to convey information. You will be giving a talk about a hobby, preparing a fact file about a wild animal and writing entries for an *A–Z of Sports*.

# My Hobby

'I support Man. United. My hobby is collecting everything about them – books, Man U. T-shirts, old programmes and autographed photos of the players.' Winston

'I go to judo every week. I've been going for three years now. It's great fun. It's good exercise and you learn how to defend yourself.' Suzette

'My hobby is gardening. I help my grandad with his allotment. He's teaching me how to grow all kinds of vegetables and flowers, and how to grow things from seeds.' Lester

# Speaking and Listening

1 In groups, take it in turns to tell each other about hobbies you had when you were younger, and what your hobbies are now. Explain:
   - what your hobby is;
   - how you got interested in it;
   - how much time you spend on it;
   - how much it costs.

   Choose someone to act as reporter and to tell the rest of the class about your group's hobbies.

2 Study the advice on page 17–18 about preparing and giving a talk. Prepare and deliver a talk to the class about your hobby.

# Preparing a Talk

Plan your talk in stages.

## Stage 1: Collecting ideas

Think of all the different things you could tell people about your hobby. Either make a list or draw a spider diagram of your ideas. On the right is the diagram Terry drew.

How to catch a fish

Where to go fishing

Fishing tackle

**FISHING**

Bait

Competitions

Funny story – catching the boot

Different types of fish

## Stage 2:
## Planning your talk

Your talk should have three parts: the beginning, the main body of the talk, the ending.

### 1 The beginning

This should be something that will grab the attention of your audience. A good way of starting your talk is to tell an exciting or funny story about your hobby.

Here is how Terry decided to begin his talk:

66 The great thing about fishing as a hobby is that you never know what's going to happen next. The funniest thing that's happened when I've been fishing is when I was convinced I'd caught something really big. But when I pulled the hook out of the water, there was an old wellington boot dangling on the end. 99

### 2 The main body of your talk

This should consist of all the information you want to give about your hobby. Look at the ideas you came up with in Stage 1 and list the information in the order you are going to give it in your talk.

Here is the order in which Terry decided to give his information on fishing:

1. Introduction – Catching the boot.
2. Where I go fishing.
3. Different types of coarse fish. (pictures from magazines)
4. My fishing tackle. (my rod, hooks, nets)
5. Bait. (box of maggots)
6. How you catch a fish.
7. Fishing competitions. (photo of cup)

### 3 The ending

This should be something that rounds off the talk, so that it doesn't come to an abrupt end. A good way of ending is to talk about your plans for the future.

Here is how Terry ended his talk:

66 It's my ambition to win first prize in the young anglers' section in the competition that our angling club runs every year. 99

# Stage 3:
## Drafting your talk

- As you are writing the draft of your talk, try to think of points in the talk when you can tell stories about any amusing or exciting things that have happened. It will help to keep your audience interested if you include stories in your talk.

- When you have finished drafting your talk, go through it and mark any places where you are going to hold up a picture or show how to use a piece of equipment.

- When you are drafting your talk, you will want to write some parts of it out in full. But where you are sure that you know what you are going to say, you can just write down headings, for example, 'Story of the biggest fish I've ever caught'.

Here is part of the draft of Terry's talk:

> There are lots of different kinds and sizes of hooks. They are usually made of steel wire and the sizes vary from 1 to 24. The larger numbers are for the smallest sizes. So a size 1 is much larger than a size 24.
>
> Some hooks are tied on to the line when you buy it. Here's a line with a hook already tied to it. *(Show example)* It's called a hook-to-nylon. This is an eyed hook. *(Show example)* To fix on an eyed hook you have to thread the line through the eye, like you thread a needle. The other sort is a spade-end hook, which you tie on, but I haven't got any of those.

# Stage 4:
## Delivering your talk

Here are some DOs and DON'Ts when delivering a talk:

- Do speak clearly and loudly. Don't mumble.

- Do look at the people who are listening to you. Don't spend all your time looking down at your script.

- Do stand up straight and stand still. Don't stand with your hands in your pockets or shuffle about.

- Don't talk too fast or too slowly. Speak at your normal pace.

- Don't speak in exactly the same tone throughout the talk. Vary the tone of your voice.

- Keep the talk flowing as smoothly as possible. Avoid hesitating and saying things such as 'Er ...' or 'Um ...'.

- Don't drop your voice at the end of the talk. End the talk with a confident statement.

- Don't get flustered if you make a mistake. Take a deep breath and start that part of your talk again.

# Marking your talks

- Take it in turns to deliver your talks.

- Use a mark sheet like the one below to record your views of each other's talks. Work in pairs and award marks out of five for the different features of each talk. You need to think about:

  1 **Structure.** Did it have a beginning, a middle and an end? Did it have a good start and a good ending?

  2 **Interest.** Was the talk interesting? Did it give you a lot of information?

  3 **Volume and clarity.** Could you hear every word? Did the speaker talk loudly and clearly enough?

  4 **Delivery.** Did the speaker hold your attention, for example, by looking at you, by showing you pictures, by varying the tone of their voice or by not fidgeting and not hesitating?

- After each talk, hold a class discussion. Say what you thought was good about the person's talk. Tell them what marks you gave them and why. Suggest what they could do to get higher marks next time they have to give a talk.

| NAME | STRUCTURE Was it well organised, with a good start and a good ending? | ?/5 | INTEREST Was it interesting and full of information? | ?/5 | VOLUME AND CLARITY Was it loud and clear enough? | ?/5 | DELIVERY Did the speaker hold your attention? | ?/5 |
|---|---|---|---|---|---|---|---|---|
|  |  |  |  |  |  |  |  |  |
|  |  |  |  |  |  |  |  |  |
|  |  |  |  |  |  |  |  |  |

Jodi's talk on meditation seems to have gone down very well....

19

# Fact File – Wolves

## WOLVES IN FOCUS

- There are two different species of wolf. One is the grey wolf, also called the timber wolf, which lives in North America, the Arctic and northern Europe. The other is the red wolf, which lives only in south-central USA.

- Wolves may go for several days without food, but after a kill they may eat up to half their body weight of meat in one go.

- Wolves can be extremely fierce. When they hunt in packs they can kill very large animals such as moose or elks, but they also hunt on their own, when they can kill animals as large as deer.

- Wolves are not always ferocious, however. There is good reason to believe that some wolves have even brought up human children. In India, for example, a girl was looked after by wolves until she was nine.

- In history and legend, the wolf has been a symbol of courage, ferocity and hardiness. The twin boys who founded the city of Rome are said to have been reared by a wolf. The English warrior Beowulf made 'wolf' part of his name.

- The grey wolf is nearly a metre high and weighs about 70 kilos. The red wolf is much smaller and lighter.

- The wolf is not a fast runner, but it can run for very long distances without stopping. A red wolf in Oklahoma was recorded as travelling over four mountain ranges in two weeks, a total of 200 kilometres (125 miles)!

- A wolf howls to warn other wolf packs that it is in the area. This is intended to prevent any chance meetings that could lead to fights.

- Wolf cubs are born deaf and blind, although they are covered with fur. For the first few weeks they are totally dependent on their mother. Only at about 18 months are they able to fend for themselves.

Wolf cubs are born deaf and blind and helpless. At 18 months old they are ferocious killers.

# Reading and Writing

In pairs, read the article about wolves (page 20). Then look at the statements below. Some are *true* and some are *false.* Look at the article and decide which are true and which are false. Then form groups and compare your answers.

1 The grey wolf is found in more places than the red wolf.

2 The red wolf is larger than the grey wolf.

3 When a wolf is angry, the hairs on its neck stand up.

4 Wolves can kill animals that are larger than them.

5 Wolves can run very fast.

6 Wolves can keep on running for hours and hours.

7 Wolves cannot go for long without food.

8 Wolf cubs are born with their eyes open.

9 Wolf cubs only stay with their parents for a short time.

10 Wolves are savage and will always attack children.

# Research and Writing

Work in pairs and prepare your own fact file page about a wild animal. Prepare your article in stages.

## Stage 1

Choose a wild animal that lives either in Britain or anywhere else in the world. Find out all you can about it from books and CD-ROMs in the school library and local library.

## Stage 2

Use these headings to make notes of what you learn about the animal:

- where it is found
- its appearance
- its home
- its food
- its young and how it looks after them
- its habits
- any special features.

## Stage 3

Select the ten most interesting facts about the animal. Decide what order you are going to put the facts in and draft two or three sentences about each fact.

## Stage 4

Find a suitable picture of the animal to include on your page. You could either photocopy one from a book, cut one out of an old magazine or draw one.

## Stage 5

Design the layout for your page. Look at how the page about wolves is laid out and how one of the facts about them is highlighted by being put in a box. Choose one fact about your animal that you could highlight, and think about where to put it on the page.

## Stage 6

Produce your page. You could either do this on a large sheet of paper to put up as part of a wall display or use a desk-top publishing package to produce a page on a computer.

# An A–Z of Sports

> A–Z of Sports is a book that gives you basic information about different sports and how they are played. Here are two entries from the book, one about ice hockey and one about badminton.

## Badminton

Badminton is usually played indoors. Two players (singles) or two couples (doubles) hit a shuttlecock over a net stretched across the playing court. The aim is to hit the shuttle so that it cannot be returned by the other player. It must go over the net and land inside the court. The winner of a game is the first player to reach 15 points (11 for women).

The rackets are similar to tennis rackets but with smaller heads and thinner handles. They are very light. The shuttle is also very light. It is usually made of plastic and slows down very quickly when it has been hit. Its flight is different from that of a ball, and of course it does not bounce.

A good badminton player is someone who can quickly judge the fall of the slowing shuttle and reach it before it hits the ground. It is a very subtle and varied game, where big hits and gentle lobs all play a part.

## Ice hockey

Ice hockey is a six-a-side game played on skates on an ice rink. Each player has a stick and the aim is to score into the opposing goal. Instead of a ball, a small flat rubber disc called the 'puck' is used.

The rink is surrounded by waist-high boards. The puck can bounce off these and still be in play, so the game flows continuously and quickly with few stoppages. Players must be expert skaters. They use short, high skates and can turn and accelerate with great skill.

It is a fast, exciting and rough game. There are frequent collisions both between players and against the barrier boards. Players wear padding and the goal-minders wear extra protection, including face masks.

Most ice hockey matches are played indoors. There are usually three 20-minute periods, separated by two 18-minute intervals.

# Speaking and Listening

Study the article on ice hockey (page 22). In pairs, make a list of the key facts that it tells you about:

1 how many players there are

2 where ice hockey is played

3 the aim of the game

4 what equipment you need for the game

5 how long matches are

6 the skills you need to play ice hockey

7 the type of game ice hockey is.

Then compare your lists in either a group or class discussion.

# Writing

Each choose a sport and draft an entry about it for an *A–Z of Sports*. Your entry should be about the same length as the entries on badminton and ice hockey. It should explain:

- how many players are needed
- where the game is played
- the aim of the game
- what equipment is needed
- how long any matches are
- how the winner is decided
- what skills players need.

When you have finished your draft, get a friend to check that you have included all the basic information and to help you to check your spelling and punctuation. Then either copy it out neatly or print out a copy, so that you can put all your entries together in a class *A–Z of Sports*.

# Reading and Writing

Read the article on badminton (page 22). Here are some statements about badminton. Some of them are *true*. Some of them are *false*. Study the information given in the article and decide which ones are true and which are false.

1 Badminton is usually played outdoors.

2 You can have two or four players.

3 You use a special ball called a shuttlecock.

4 The aim is to catch the shuttle when it is hit to you.

5 The shuttlecock must go over the net and land inside the court.

6 The winner is the first to get 15 points.

7 A badminton racket is heavier than a tennis racket.

8 Shuttlecocks are usually made of plastic.

9 A shuttlecock travels through the air in the same way as a ball.

10 Good players can judge the flight of the shuttlecock.

# Alphabetical order

- Arrange the entries in your *A–Z of Sports* in alphabetical order according to the first, second and third letters of each word.

- On your own, put the following sports in alphabetical order:

**cricket rugby athletics fencing volleyball archery football baseball skiing tennis badminton judo golf swimming boxing skating gymnastics bowling cycling.**

In this unit you will be expressing your opinions about pop groups and pop shows, and writing reviews of CDs. You will also be talking about the kind of books you like, and reading and writing book reviews.

# My Kind of Music

On the right is a list of different types of music. Put the list in alphabetical order and then put a circle round the type of music you like best.

punk   indie   classical   soul   reggae
blues   rock   folk   pop   heavy metal
opera   dance/house   grunge   jazz
rhythm and blues    country and western

Now do a class survey to find out what music other people in the class like. Make a chart like the one class 8Z made (right).

| Our favourite music | |
| --- | --- |
| Dance/House | ● ● ● ● |
| Grunge | ● |
| Heavy Metal | ● ● ● |
| Indie | ● ● ● ● ● |
| Pop | ● ● ● ● ● ● ● ● ● ● ● ● |
| Rock | ● ● ● ● |
| Soul | ● ● |

## Speaking, Listening and Writing

- Below, three people give their opinions about the groups they like. In pairs, tell each other which is your favourite group and why.

- On your own, write a paragraph about 'My Favourite Pop Group'. Say what type of songs they sing and why you like them.

'I like The Beatles, because they wrote good songs. People still sing them today. No other group has had as many great number 1 hits. It's so sad that John Lennon was killed, otherwise they may all have got together again.'
– Penny

'Bon Jovi have been around for a long time and Jon Bon Jovi is my hero. They are Canadian, so they don't always get very high in the British charts. But I think 'Bed of Roses' is the most wonderful song I've ever heard.'
– Paul

'I think the Spice Girls are fabulous. Their routines are fantastic and their songs are really catchy.'
– Sam

# TV Pop Shows

What makes a good pop show on TV? Here are some different opinions.

'The best programmes always give you the latest chart details.'

'You need a good presenter. Someone with lots of personality, who is always cracking jokes and making you laugh.'

'The best shows have bands performing live and create a real disco

'A good show has plenty of video clips in it.'

'I like programmes that have interviews and give you lots of facts about the stars.'

'The best shows concentrate just on the music and you don't have other things like cartoons in them.'

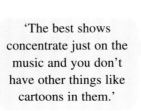

## Speaking and Listening

- In groups, discuss the pop shows that are on TV at the moment.
- Which ones do you like and which do you dislike? Give your reasons.
- What makes a good TV pop show? Make a list of the features of a good TV pop show.
- Imagine you are a group of people planning a new TV pop show, which is to be shown at 7.00 p.m. on Thursday evenings. Think of a title for your show and plan what it will include. Then choose someone to report your ideas to the rest of the class in a class discussion. Discuss which group has the best ideas for a new pop programme.

# CD Reviews

A CD review is a piece of writing that tells you about the CD. A review should tell you several things about the CD:

- the title of the CD and the name of the band or singer;
- what sort of music is on the CD;
- how good the writer thinks the CD is and how much they think you will like it.

The review below was in *Shout* magazine.

TIP FOR THE TOP

Watch out for **Niall, Alan, Adam** and **Glen** – they're **OTT** and they're going to be huge! The lads are already massive in their native Ireland and we're sure they're going to follow up that success here very soon. Listen out for their fab debut single, 'Let Me In', out this month. We can never have too many boy bands!

## Speaking and Listening

1 In groups, talk about the CDs you like at the moment and about any new bands and new CDs you have heard. Say what you think makes the CD special and why you like the group. Talk about who is in the group, how they dress and how they perform. Say what you like about the song – is it the music or is it the words? Is there anything else that makes this CD special?

2 Imagine that you work for a radio show which reviews the latest releases. Each choose a CD and write a short review of it, like the review from *Shout* (above). Then tape-record your own *Tips for the Top* programme in which you read your reviews and introduce the CDs that you like.

# Chartbusters

Here are two special reviews that were written by students of your own age. They are special because you won't have heard of either of the groups!

## Let's Hear it for the Yee-Hahs!

Forget the Spice Girls and all those other trendy bands, let's get back to good old Country and Western, where the real music is. That's exactly what the Yee-Hahs have done. They hit the charts a week ago with their new album Hurdy Gurdy Girl, and my bet is they won't stop till they hit the top - with a Yee-Hah!

Lead singer Mop (her childhood nickname - real name Maudie) grew up on a ranch in Carolina with sister Jo who plays guitar. Brother Charlie plays the accordion and cousin Pete writes all the songs. He says he gets his inspiration while out riding the range and rounding up the cattle. Rather him than me! This latest album is a wonderful mixture from the twanging beat of 'Run from the Lasso' to the haunting melody of 'Mellow Moons', a slow smoochy number about their beloved Carolina. Let's hear it for the Yee-Hahs! You haven't heard the last of them!

Robin

## I'm Fanatical about Fanatical

If you haven't heard the new album Crimson by Fanatical, then hurry down to the shops now, and snap it up! It includes all their best songs, including their number 1 hit 'Terminal Velocity' and their absolutely brilliant new single 'It's Cruel Out There'.

This is certainly the best début album I've ever heard. If you're thinking Fanatical's heavy-type music isn't for you, then just try listening to some of the slower numbers, like 'Meet Me Half-way'. You'll get a real surprise. Joe Layton's singing just gets better and better.

I suppose you could say I'm fanatical about Fanatical. Definitely a big 10 out of 10!

Jasmin

# Writing

You won't have heard of either Fanatical or the Yee-Hahs because Jasmin and Robin invented them!

Invent a group of your own. Give the group a name. Decide how many people there are in the group and what sort of music they play. Think up a name for their new album and for their latest hits. Then write a review of their new CD in the way that Jasmin and Robin have done.

# Book Reviews

These book reviews appeared in a newspaper for young people.

## Family Fortunes –
### Books about the ups and downs of family life

### Robopop
by Emma Laybourn

Move over Terminator, meet Tarragon! Ben's father is a robotics boffin – when he has to go to a conference during half-term, he leaves a disaster-prone robot in his place. Seriously funny techno mishaps follow.

### The Snake-stone
by Berlie Doherty

James has just three things to remind him of his real mother – some baby clothes she made for him, a snake-stone and a note. But he can't stop wondering about her and why she gave him up. Don't miss this gripping story to find out.

### Puppy Fat
by Morris Gleitzman

Keith's got his worrying head on again. His parents are separated and they are letting themselves go badly. Mum watches telly every night in an old housecoat and bedsocks and Dad's got a wobbly bottom and saggy tum. But Keith's determined to get them into shape. You'll love this funny and moving story by Morris Gleitzman.

### The Divorce Express
by Paula Danziger

Every weekend 14-year-old Phoebe leaves her dad in the country and rides the bus, nicknamed the Divorce Express, to visit her mum in New York. She's lonely and miserable until she makes friends with Rosie, who catches the same bus. A brilliant story about learning to cope with family

break-up.

### Dancing Through the Shadows
by Theresa Thomlinson

Ellie's family life seems shattered when she discovers that her mother has breast cancer. But with the help of friends and her love of dancing, she is able to face what appears to be a bleak future. A heart-warming story about a family crisis.

# Reading and Writing

Read the book reviews, then write down the answers to these questions.

**1** Which book is about a girl who loves dancing?

**2** In which book does the boy's father design robots?

**3** Which book tells the story of a girl whose mother lives in New York?

**4** In which book is there a father who is letting himself grow fat?

**5** Which book tells a story about a boy whose mother gave him up when he was a baby?

**6** In which book do the main events happen at half-term?

**7** In which book is the girl's mother dying of cancer?

**8** In which two books are the parents of the main character separated?

**9** Why is Paula Danziger's book called *The Divorce Express*?

**10** Why is Berlie Doherty's book called *The Snake-stone*?

# Speaking and Listening

**1** On your own, put the five books in order, starting with the one you'd most like to read and ending with the one you think would be the most boring.

Then, in groups, show each other your lists and explain the reasons for your choice.

**2** Suzanne read a book called *The Snowman*. Read what she said about it below.

In your groups, talk about the types of stories you enjoy reading. Then tell each other about a book you have read recently.

> **"** I liked a Point Horror book called *The Snowman*. The main character is Heather. Her parents died when she was a baby and her uncle treats her very badly. Heather's parents left her lots of money, but her evil uncle won't let her have a penny. He makes her work in a greasy café. This is when Heather meets the snowman – a boy with white hair – and the story really begins … I just couldn't put the book down. **"**

# Reading

A book review should tell you four things:

- what type of book it is;
- who the main characters are;
- some details of the plot, so that you know what the book is about;
- how good the book is and how much you are likely to enjoy it.

Study Alastair's review of *The Back House Ghosts* (below). Notice how it is divided into paragraphs. As you read it, work out which paragraphs tell you about:

- the plot and what type of story it is;
- the characters;
- how good the book is.

### The Back House Ghosts by A. Silcott

This book is about Ellen who lives in a guest house with her mother and her sister Bella. One day her mother makes a mistake and overbooks the guest house. So Ellen and Bella have to go and sleep in the Back House, an outbuilding which isn't used any more.

Ellen starts seeing and hearing strange things in the Back House. So she starts to wonder who this person is that won't leave her alone. What is it that it wants to tell her, so that it can rest once and for all? Ellen's curiosity gets her into all kinds of trouble, but she won't stop until she has found out the truth.

I like Ellen's character best, because she is always wondering and because she always seems to get out of a tight spot. She has a lot of determination to find out the truth, and nearly kills herself at the same time.

This book is a gripping ghost story, which keeps you on the edge of your seat all the way through.

Alastair

# Writing

Now write a review of a book you have read. Plan to write four paragraphs. In paragraphs 1 and 2 explain what sort of story it is and who the main characters are, and give some details of the plot. In paragraph 3 say which character(s) you liked and why. In paragraph 4 say how good the book is and whether you think other people would enjoy it.

# Four Hints to Improve Your Spelling

## Hint 1: Read your work through carefully

Before you hand in a piece of written work, read it through to check your spellings. If you are unsure about a word, either look it up in a dictionary or ask someone how to spell it correctly.

## Hint 2: Keep a spelling book

When your teacher shows you that you have made a mistake, write the correct spelling of the word in your spelling book. Then use the Look-Focus-Say-Cover-Write-Check method to help you to learn it (see *English Direct* Book 1, page 21).

## Hint 3: Look out for letter patterns

Many words in English have the same letter patterns at either the beginning or the end.

There are many words that end in **-ight**, for example:

*light, night, might.*

Work with a partner and make a list of words that end in **-ight**. You could start with these:

**1** A word that means held firmly and securely.

**2** A word that describes the action of flying.

**3** A situation in which people try to hit or hurt each other.

**4** A sudden feeling of fear.

**5** A word that means the ability to see.

## Hint 4: Learn spelling rules

Although there are exceptions to most English spelling rules, spelling rules can be helpful.

The most well-known spelling rule in English is that **'i' goes before 'e' except after 'c'** (when the sound is long 'ee'). For example:

*field, besiege* but *receipt.*

This works for most words, but there are a few exceptions, for example:

*weird, seize, protein.*

♪♫ Good night ♫ Sleep tight ♪ ♫ Hope the bugs don't bight!

Don't you mean bite?

# ROOSTER BOOSTER
PAXO

In this unit you will be looking at how people try to persuade you to do things or to buy things. You will be studying advertisements, and writing and designing your own advertisements.

# Tricks of the Trade

Advertisers use a number of methods to try to persuade you to do things or buy things.

**1 Pictures**

They choose pictures that make things look attractive.

**2 Slogans**

They use words and phrases that will catch your attention and stick in your mind. These are called **slogans**. A slogan is often printed in capitals as a heading. Another way of making words stand out is to underline them or to print them in a different type, such as **bold type** or *italics*.

*Beanz Meanz Heinz*

**3 Descriptive words**

Advertisers also use lots of descriptive words to make things seem attractive. Often they choose words to exaggerate how good something is. Instead of just saying that something is 'good', they say that it is 'brilliant', 'wonderful' or 'magnificent'.

## Speaking and Listening

1 In pairs, read and study the advertisement for Oakwood Theme Park (page 33). Make lists of things that there are to do at Oakwood:

- for teenagers
- for older people
- for very young children.

2 In groups, compare your lists. Then talk about how the advertisement tries to persuade you that Oakwood is an exciting place to visit.

- How do the pictures suggest that a visit to Oakwood would be fun?
- Pick out the slogans that are used in the advertisement. What do the slogans suggest about Oakwood?
- Make a list of ten words that are used to suggest that you would enjoy a visit to Oakwood.

Choose someone to report your ideas to the rest of the class and share your ideas in a class discussion.

# '8 Miles of Rides, 80 Acres of Fun'

In all, there are 40 different rides and attractions to enjoy. Including Europe's biggest (and scariest!) wooden roller coaster, Megafobia. Water rides – like the swirling tubes of Snake River Falls. The Pirate Ship. The Bobsleigh Run. Nutty Jake's Gold Mine. Go Karting...Even a boating lake and a putting range – so you can relax between adventures.

From hair raising rides to furry farm animals, Oakwood is tremendous fun for everyone from tots to teens to grannies. It's not just Wales' largest theme park, it's a magical world, packed full of thrills and adventure, that starts from the moment you step inside.

Younger children will feel right at home in Playtown. There are lots of rides and games offering big fun for the little ones. And they'll especially love cuddling the furry friends at Playtown Farm.

But whatever your age, you're never too old for Oakwood. There's just so much for all the family to enjoy. In fact, one visit just isn't enough, and you'll want to come back for more and more and more and...

# Adjectives

A **noun** is the name of anything –
An <u>apple</u>, a <u>girl</u>, a <u>bird</u>, a <u>ring</u>.

An **adjective** tells you about a noun –
<u>Little</u> or <u>happy</u> or <u>sparkling</u> or <u>brown</u>.

An **adjective** is a word that tells you more about a noun.

Advertisers often use adjectives to suggest that something is worth doing or buying. For example:

- Try it! The taste is <u>delicious</u>.
- It's a <u>brilliant</u> day out for everyone!
- It is a <u>tremendous</u> film.

## Reading

Below is an advertisement for another theme park called Thorpe Park. Some of the adjectives have been left out and are listed on the left.

In pairs, study the advertisement and work out which word fits in which gap. Make a list of the words you choose, then compare your list with the list other pairs have made.

| | |
|---|---|
| biggest | adventurous |
| marvellous | fantastic |
| superb | greatest |
| fabulous | thrilling |
| brilliant | amazing |

For a ___1___ fun-filled day out, take a trip to **Thorpe Park!** There's loads of ___2___ things to see and do including family favourites like the ___3___ log flume ride **Loggers Leap** – one of the highest plunges in the UK, and the ___4___ **Thunder River** – the only rapid ride in the south of England.

There's also a traditional 1930s working farm, as well as **Fantasy Reef** – a ___5___ sandy beach area with shallow fun pools, water jets and slides. Also don't miss the ___6___ **X:\ No Way Out.** This is **Thorpe Park's** ___7___ and most ___8___ ride yet. As you plummet backwards in total darkness, it'll give you the ___9___ scare of your life!

You're guaranteed a ___10___ day out at **Thorpe Park.**

# Writing

# Corton Park

Imagine that a new theme park called Corton Park is about to open. It is your job to design the leaflet to advertise the park. Work with a partner to produce the leaflet. Plan your leaflet in stages.

## Stage 1: Making a list of the attractions

What attractions are there at Corton Park? (You could get some ideas by looking at the illustrations on this page.) Make a list of all the things there are to do at Corton Park. Make sure there are things for:

● teenagers

● very young children

● older people.

## Stage 2: Planning the layout of your leaflet

Plan the layout of your leaflet on a blank sheet of paper. Think about what pictures you are going to include and where you are going to put them. Decide where your headings should go and where the writing is going to go.

## Stage 3: Drafting the advertisement

Think up some slogans that will catch people's attention and stick in their minds. Use them as headings, then write the advertisement using lots of adjectives to make everything at the park seem fun.

## Stage 4: Revising and redrafting your advertisements

Show the draft of your advertisement to some other pairs. Discuss which parts of your advertisements work well. Suggest one or two things that each of you could change in order to make your advertisements even better.

## Stage 5: Checking for mistakes

Check your advertisement to make sure that what you have written makes complete sense. Check that there are no spelling and punctuation mistakes.

## Stage 6: Producing the leaflet

Make a copy of the leaflet to put on the display board. You could either make a hand-written copy or use a word processor to produce a printed copy.

# Selling a Product

Advertisers use words and pictures to create an image for their product. They want their words and pictures to suggest that you will feel better or get better value by using their product.

# Speaking and Listening

In groups, study the advert for Boots ACT (page 36) and discuss these questions:

**1** What does the advertisement suggest about people who use Boots ACT?

**2** Talk about the picture. What does the picture suggest?

**3** What slogans does the advertisement use? What do the slogans suggest?

**4** Do you think it is a successful advertisement? Give your reasons.

Choose someone to report your ideas to the rest of the class, and share your ideas in a class discussion.

Advertisers also choose names for their products that will help to create a particular image of the product. These names are called **brand names**, because a particular type of something is called a brand.

# Writing

**1** In pairs, imagine that you work for a rival company which has produced a new treatment for spots. Choose a name for it, such as 'Zap-it', and design an advert for it to go in a teenage magazine.

**2** On your own, imagine that a sports company has asked you to design a magazine advertisement for one of its new products, either 'Hot-Shot Football Boots' or 'Speedo Running Shoes'. The advert is to go in a sports magazine for teenagers.

You need to think about:

● the picture you are going to use and the image you want the picture to give;

● a slogan that will get your message across in a few words and that will stick in people's minds;

● words to describe your product that will suggest that it is the best one on the market.

Produce a draft of your advertisement, then form groups and compare your ideas. Decide which people in your group have the best ideas, then share your ideas in a class discussion.

# Speaking and Listening

In groups, study the names of the chocolate bars shown in the illustration on the right.

**1** Discuss what image of each chocolate bar is created by its particular name.

**2** Make lists of the brand names of different types of car. Talk about the image of the car that is created by its name.

# TV Adverts

TV advertisements can use music as well as words and pictures to create an image of a product.

## Speaking and Listening

In groups, watch a number of TV adverts for different products.
Then discuss these questions:

1 Which adverts tell a story? Which one has the best storyline?

2 What sort of pictures (for example, of people and places) are used in the adverts? What image of the products do these pictures suggest?

3 Which adverts use slogans? Which advert has the best slogan?

4 Which adverts use music? What sort of music do they use and what does that music suggest about the product?

5 Which adverts are aimed at young people? Which adverts are aimed at older people? How can you tell?

6 Which advert do you think works best? Say why.

## Writing

Choose one of the adverts you have seen and write four or five sentences about it, saying why you thought it was a good advert.

# Planning

Imagine that your group has been asked to plan a four-frame TV advert for a new product – a new breakfast cereal, a new soft drink or a new healthcare product. Plan a storyboard for the advert (Natalie's is shown below).

- Choose a suitable *name* for your product.
- Think up a *slogan* you can use in the advert.
- Decide which *age group* you are going to aim your advert at.
- Think about the *image* you want to give of your product.

Then discuss how you are going to create that image.

- Are you going to focus on the product or will the advert tell a story?
- Will you show people in the advert? What will they be doing?
- Will they speak or will you use a **voice-over** (an off-screen voice that tells or comments on the story)?
- Will you use any background music? If so, what sort of music will it be?

# Writing and Drawing

When you have finished discussing your ideas, produce your storyboard.

1 Make rough drawings in the four frames to show what pictures will appear on the screen.
2 Write speech bubbles for anything that people say.
3 Write in any words or captions that appear on the screen.
4 Write in any words that will be spoken as voice-overs.
5 Write in details of any music you are going to use.

# Selling your Skateboard

If you want to sell your skateboard – or anything else – you can put an advert in a shop window. The advert should contain the following key pieces of information:

- a description of the object;
- details of its condition, for example, how old it is;
- the price you are asking for it;
- how to contact you, for example, your telephone number and/or address.

Below are some examples of adverts that were put in a shop window.

### WALKMAN FOR SALE

complete with headphones and two cassette tapes

fair condition

good value at only £6.00

PHONE 0370 605158

### FOR SALE
blue denim jacket
good condition
(only 6 months old)
popular brand name
price £15

### FOR SALE

A bargain at £50
Stormbuster 4 Tent
Almost New
Ring **01646 600122** for further details

### FOR SALE

Boy's Mountain Bike
good condition, 12 gears,
metallic blue
free bike pump with it!!!
any sensible offers considered
phone (day) 01437 762924
       (eve) 01437 837501

## Speaking and Listening

In pairs, study the adverts (above) which appeared in a shop window. Then discuss these questions:

- Which advert conveys the information most clearly?
- Which advert is the most eye-catching?
- Which advert misses out some key information?

## Writing

Imagine that you have something you want to sell because you no longer use it, for example, a bicycle, a pair of ice skates or some computer games. Write an advertisement to put in a shop window.

- Use a computer to make your advertisement as eye-catching as possible.
- Ask a friend to help you to check your advert for mistakes.

# Spelling: Adding -ing and -ed to Verbs

In the first unit (page 13) you learned how verbs have different tenses.

Sometimes we use the present tense:
*I walk to school. I am walking to school.*

Sometimes we use the past tense:
*I walked to school. I was walking to school.*

When you add -ing or -ed to the verb *walk* it does not change its spelling. Many other verbs do not change their spelling when you add -ing or -ed, for example:

*look, looked, looking
laugh, laughed, laughing.*

However, some groups of verbs do change their spelling when you add -ing or -ed. Here are some rules to help you with verbs that do change their spelling. But remember, there are always some exceptions to rules like these.

## Rule 1

Many verbs that end in -e lose the letter e when you add -ing or -ed. For example:

*smile, smiled, smiling
move, moved, moving
argue, argued, arguing.*

## Rule 2

Some verbs are short words of one syllable, ending in a single consonant, for example, *slip* or *wag*. These words double the consonant when -ing or -ed are added, for example:

*slip, slipped, slipping
wag, wagged, wagging.*

## Rule 3

Some verbs end in a consonant followed by a -y, for example, *cry.* These words change the y to an i before -ed, but keep the y before -ing. For example:

*cry, cried, crying
terrify, terrified, terrifying.*

## Writing

Copy out this passage, adding either -ing or -ed to the verbs in brackets.

I was (walk) down the street, when I (trip) up. I (bang) my elbow and (cry) out in pain. My arm was (bleed) and my shirt was (rip). A woman was (come) towards me. She put down the bags she was (carry) and (help) me up. Then she (call) an ambulance.

# Colour Poems

**In this unit** you will be looking at poems in which comparisons are made. You will be writing your own poems using comparisons. There are also some poems for you to read aloud and perform.

Sometimes when we talk about colours we use **comparisons.**

For example, we say that something is as green as the grass or as blue as the sky. Or we say that somebody was as white as a sheet or as red as a beetroot.

Below is a poem about colours which uses several comparisons. The writer imagines a boy who is blind talking about colours. Because he is blind, the boy uses his other senses to describe the colours.

## Speaking and Listening

In pairs, take it in turns to read the poem on the right aloud to each other, then discuss these questions.

1 What sound does the boy say is like **a)** green, **b)** blue, **c)** red?

2 What smell does he say pink is like?

3 What does he say purple is like?

4 What does he say white is like?

5 Which of the lines in the poem make the best comparison? Explain why.

## Writing

Choose a colour and write your own poem, which tries to describe the colour by comparing it to things you hear, smell, taste or touch. On the right is an example of such a poem.

### I Asked the Little Boy Who Cannot See

I asked the little boy who cannot see,
'And what is colour like?'
'Why, green,' said he,
'Is like the rustle when the wind blows through
The forest; running water, that is blue;
And red is like a trumpet sound; and pink
Is like the smell of roses; and I think
That purple must be like a thunderstorm;
And yellow is like something soft and warm;
And white is a pleasant stillness when you
Lie and dream.'

### Yellow

Yellow is like a soft, whispering voice.
It is like the smell of a cornfield at harvest time.
It is like the sweet taste of soft ice cream.
It is like the sun on your skin in summer.
*Jenny*

# Opposites Poems

The poem below is about adjectives that are opposites. It uses comparisons to show the difference between them.

### Opposites

As soft as silk, as hard as stone.
As wet as rain, as dry as a bone.
As fast as a cheetah, as slow as a snail.
As short as a pin, as long as a whale.
As white as a sheet, as black as coal.
As deaf as a post, as blind as a mole.
As round as a ball, as square as a box.
As silly as a sheep, as cunning as a fox.
As hot as an oven, as cold as ice.
As loud as a scream, as quiet as mice.

*Anon*

# Writing

Work in pairs and draft your own opposites poem by changing each of the lines in the poem **'Opposites'** (above). Do not worry about making your poem rhyme.

Here are the first two lines of the opposites poem that Tracy and Ravinda wrote:

As soft as a pillow, as hard as an iron bar.
As wet as a teardrop, as dry as an empty bucket.

Now try to write your own opposites poem, like the one Emma wrote (on the right).

As slow as a hedgehog plodding across the road.
As fast as a bullet speeding towards me.
As loud as a fire alarm bleeping and beeping.
As quiet as the night all silent and calm.
As hot as the toaster that browns my waffles.
As cold as the ice cube that freezes my drink.
As sharp as the needle that pricked my finger.
As blunt as a snapped pencil.

# Similes

A statement that compares one thing to another is called a **simile**. The words 'like' or 'as' are generally used to introduce the comparison.

Here are some examples of similes:

*The shark's teeth are like a row of daggers.*

*She ran as fast as a deer.*

## Writing

Complete these similes by using the comparisons that are listed below. The first one has been done for you.

**1** The boom of thunder sounded like …

*The boom of thunder sounded like a bomb exploding.*

**2** She crept along the street like …

**3** The white clouds looked like …

**4** The monster's claws were as sharp as …

**5** The full moon was as bright as …

**6** The hamster's eyes were like …

**7** The football flew into the net like …

**8** The aeroplane sped across the sky like …

**9** He trembled with fear like …

**10** The cave walls were as wet as …

**11** He howled with pain like …

**12** The angry teacher strode across the room like …

| | |
|---|---|
| a bullet | a golden coin |
| razor blades | a frightened rabbit |
| a wounded animal | a prowling fox |
| a silver arrow | the scales of a fish |
| a charging buffalo | small black buttons |
| a bomb exploding | pieces of cotton wool |

*Sarah ran as fast as a cheetah.*

*Jason rode the waves like a dolphin.*

# Simile Poems

## Writing

In his poem (right) John uses two similes to describe what his dog does when it is in different moods. Use John's poem as model and write your own simile poem about an animal or pet of some kind. Your poem should consist of five lines:

line 1 – Sometimes

line 2 – The animal you are writing about

line 3 – What the animal does

line 4 – What other person, animal or object you think it is like

line 5 – What that other person, animal or object is doing.

Sometimes
our dog
lies in the shade and sleeps
like an old man at the seaside
dozing in a deckchair.

Sometimes
our dog
prowls about the house
like a caged lion
pacing up and down in the zoo.

*John*

## Writing

1  In his poem (below) Jack uses a simile to describe one of the things that happens on a stormy day. Use Jack's poem as a model and write your own simile poem describing what else happens on a stormy day. You could write about the thunder, the lightning, the wind or the rain. Your poem should consist of four lines:

line 1 – On a stormy day

line 2 – What you are describing (the thunder, lightning, wind or rain)

line 3 – What it does

line 4 – What it is like.

2  Write another four-line simile poem in which you describe something that happens on another type of day, for example, a foggy day, a frosty day, a snowy day, a breezy day or a sunny day.

Or you could write about what happens on an autumn day, a winter day, a spring day or a summer day.

Below is what Alana wrote about an autumn day.

On an autumn day
brown leaves
fall from the trees
like crisps from an upturned packet.

*Alana*

On a stormy day
dark clouds
blot out the sun
like heavy black curtains.

*Jack*

# Drafting a Poem

## What is Strong?

As strong as
    the bulging muscles
    of a Sumo wrestler
    and his sweaty, oily body

As strong as
    the deep low growl
    of an angry lion

As strong as
    the fierce flames
    of a roaring fire-breathing dragon

As strong as
    the sharp spicy taste
    of a hot curry

As strong as
    the handshake of a giant
    gripping your fingers
    like a vice.

*Ramon*

## Speaking and Listening

In groups, discuss how Ramon uses a number of comparisons in his poem (left) to answer the question 'What is strong?' Talk about how he makes use of all five senses in the poem. In which parts of the poem does he use his sense of:

- smell
- taste
- sound
- touch
- sight?

## Writing

Choose one of the adjectives listed below. Use Ramon's poem as a model and write your own 'What is ...?' poem. Before you begin, study the rest of this chapter (pages 46–47) and draft your poem in stages, as Ramon did.

bright    soft    rough    sharp    hard    cold

tall   slow   hot   deep   wide   long

quiet   huge   smooth   heavy

## Stage 1:
### Collecting ideas

Ramon began by drawing up a list of everything that he could think of as being strong. As well as objects and materials that are strong he tried to think of animals and people that are strong. He also tried to think of a strong colour, a strong sound, a strong taste, a strong touch and a strong smell.

Look at Ramon's brainstorm on the right.

*Begin by making a list of things you connect with the word you are writing about.*

Sounds –
a lion's roar
thunder
pop groups like Nirvana

The <u>taste</u> of hot curry
a Mexican chili burger
hot peppers

People –
bodyguard
Sumo wresslers
giants

Touch –
hot water
flames

STRONG

Objects –
tanks
a rock
an iron bar

Animals –
tigers
an angry lion
guard dogs

The <u>smell</u> of manure
a sweaty body

# Stage 2:
## Making a plan and writing the first draft

Ramon picked one of the ideas and began to write a draft of his poem. On the right is his draft of the first section.

*As you write your draft, cross out words you decide to change and move words around, as Ramon did, until you think you have got it right.*

As strong as
~~a big fat bodyguard~~
the big musles
of a Sumo wressler
and his ~~smelly~~/fat body  *sweaty*
covered in oil

As strong as
~~an angry lion~~
~~growling because it's hungry~~
the ~~roaring of~~ hungry growl
of an angry lion

# Stage 3:
## Revising and redrafting

Ramon showed his friend Pavel his draft. They discussed each section of the poem together and then Ramon made some changes. On the right is the draft of the changes he made to the first section.

*Show your draft to a friend and discuss ways you could improve it.*

As strong as
                *bulging*
the ~~big~~ musles
of a Sumo wressler
                        *oily*
and his sweaty ~~oil covered~~ body

As strong as
            *deep low*
the ~~hungry~~ growl
of an angry lion

# Stage 4:
## Checking the grammar, punctuation and spelling

Next, Ramon got his teacher to help him check his work before he made a neat copy. Here are some of the spelling mistakes they found:

*musles, wressler, feirce, spicey.*

*Ask your teacher to help you to check your work before you make a neat copy.*

# Stage 5:
## Writing or printing a neat copy

Ramon used a word processor to make a neat copy of his poem, so that it could go up on the class display board.

*If you can, use a word processor to make a neat copy of your poem.*

# Poems to Read and Perform

## Useless

You're as useless
as a bucket without a hole
as a mine without some coal
as a key without a lock
as a tick without a tock.

As useless
as a sky without the birds
as a book without the words
as a glove without a hand
as a snapped elastic band.

As useless
as a curve without a bend
as a story without an end
as a punctured rubber tyre
as the promise of a liar.

As useless
as a record with a scratch
as a cancelled football match
as a fair without the fun
as a rhyme that doesn't work.

As useless
as an oil-polluted sea
as a cold cup of tea
as a gift that isn't free

In fact you're almost as useless
as me.

*Paul Higgins*

## I'm Telling You

I'm as wise as an owl.
I'm as cunning as a cat.
You're as slimy as a snail.
You're as dirty as a rat.
I'm as brave as a lion.
I'm as strong as an ox.
You're as weak as a kitten.
You're as sneaky as a fox.
I'm as bright as a button.
I'm as hard as nails.
You're as useless as a yacht
Without any sails!

*Sean Forbes*

### You!

You!
Your head is like a hollow drum.
You!
Your eyes are like balls of flame.
You!
Your ears are like fans for blowing fire.
You!
Your nostril is like a mouse's hole.
You!
Your mouth is like a lump of mud.
You!
Your hands are like drum-sticks.
You!
Your belly is like a pot of bad water.
You!
Your legs are like wooden posts.
You!
Your backside is like a mountain-top.

*Traditional African*

# Speaking and Listening

In groups, practise reading and performing these three poems.

Try different ways of reading them. For example, discuss which lines you might read with only one voice and which lines you might say together.

Take it in turns to present your performances to the rest of the class. When you have all finished, discuss whose performances worked best and why.

# Writing

1 Write a poem like 'Useless' in which you use comparisons to say how brilliant, fantastic or wonderful someone is.

2 Use the poem 'You!' as a model. Write a similar poem in which you use a number of comparisons to insult somebody.

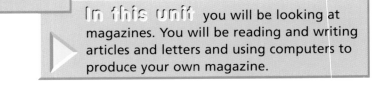

In this unit you will be looking at magazines. You will be reading and writing articles and letters and using computers to produce your own magazine.

# Teenage Magazines

'Most of the magazines are about things that girls are interested in. It's all *girls'* fashions, *girls'* health and the stories are all about *girls* meeting boys.'

Sam

'There is too much about pop stars and TV soaps. There should be more articles about things to do and places to go.'

Shameena

'I think they are good value. There are all kinds of different articles, stories and reviews to tell you what's new.'

Kalpna

'I like the readers' true experiences and the photo stories.'

Alison

'I like the problem pages. They make you realise that other people have problems like yours and tell you how to cope with them.'

Tara

'I don't read magazines except ones that are all about the subject that interests me, in my case football magazines.'

Chris

# Speaking and Listening

In groups, talk about the magazines that you read. Discuss each of the comments (above) and say why you agree or disagree with them.

Carry out a survey to find out which magazines people read and which is their favourite magazine. Ask people these questions:

- Which magazines do you read?
- What is your favourite magazine?
- Why is it your favourite magazine?

Keep a record of their answers. Then report your findings to the class in a class discussion.

# The Contents of Magazines

You can find out a lot about a magazine by studying its contents.

Tara and Kalpna looked at an issue of *Shout* magazine and made a list of the contents they found:

- Pop news and pictures
- Readers' true experiences
- Fashion articles
- Special reports
- Health and beauty articles
- Problems page
- Horoscope
- Soap gossip
- Adverts
- Letters.

Below is what they wrote about *Shout* magazine after studying its contents.

It's a magazine that's for girls, because it's got lots of fashion and beauty tips and all the letters and readers' true experiences are by girls. But boys would find some of it interesting. For example, in the issue we looked at there was a special report on joyriding. But there was nothing on football or anything like that.

# Reading and Writing

In pairs, choose a magazine to study. Make a list of its contents, like the list Tara and Kalpna made. Then write a paragraph of at least three or four sentences saying what you learned about the magazine from studying its contents.

# Speaking and Listening

In groups, imagine that you have been given the job of designing a new magazine for young people of your age. The owners want it to sell to boys as well as girls. The magazine is to be 56 pages long and will contain 8 pages of advertisements.

Discuss the different types of article you will put in the magazine. Then draw up a list of contents, saying how many pages you will give to each type of article.

When you have finished, share your ideas in a class discussion.

# Readers' True Experiences

## Five *Shout* readers tell of their spooky experiences

# The Fright of My Life

'Once when I was staying at a friend's house I was lying in bed when I saw a big black shape sort of come out of the wall. It was shaped like a person only much taller and wider. When I screamed it just disappeared. Her mum came running to find out what was wrong and I was too embarrassed to say I'd seen a ghost so I told her I'd seen a spider. But I've never gone back into her house since.'

Rachel, 9

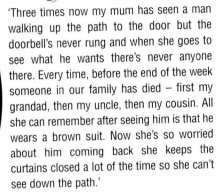

'Three times now my mum has seen a man walking up the path to the door but the doorbell's never rung and when she goes to see what he wants there's never anyone there. Every time, before the end of the week someone in our family has died – first my grandad, then my uncle, then my cousin. All she can remember after seeing him is that he wears a brown suit. Now she's so worried about him coming back she keeps the curtains closed a lot of the time so she can't see down the path.'

*Misha, 11*

'When I was younger we went to visit my gran one day and I went into the kitchen to get a biscuit. There was an old lady in there standing like she was doing the washing up at the sink. I got a fright because I didn't know anyone was in there and ran back to Gran and Mum. I told Gran I couldn't get a biscuit because her friend was in there doing the dishes, but Gran laughed and said there was no one else in the house.

'When I made them go to look there was nobody there and all the cups and things were still sitting there untouched. But after I described the lady, Gran said it could have been the ghost of her mum, my great-grandma, who was always very tidy and would've told her off for not washing up the tea things straight away!'

Leah, 12

'My Auntie Anne's cat died nearly two years ago, but often when you go round there you can still feel her brushing round your legs. My auntie left her cat basket out where it had always been, and she says that some mornings the blanket inside is still warm as if it's been sleeping there all night.'

Marie, 10

'My cousin used to have a dog that started to bite people so it had to be put down. He says that since then several people have said they've still seen his dog running round the garden, and he actually got a letter from the Post Office saying they wouldn't deliver his letters to the door until he chained up his "dangerous dog" that was running loose.

'When he rang to tell them it was only a ghost they thought it was a joke and in the end he had to get the local newspaper in to help him prove to them he was telling the truth!'

*Bernadette, 12*

# Reading

Many teenage magazines contain articles about readers' true experiences.

Read the stories on page 52. Then write down the name of the reader who tells a story about:

1 A ghost that appeared through a wall.

2 A ghost who wears a brown suit.

3 A ghost that she saw in her gran's kitchen.

4 A ghost that disappeared when she screamed.

5 A ghost that warms a blanket overnight.

6 A ghost that runs around the garden.

7 A ghost that appears when someone in the family is going to die.

8 A ghost that rubs itself against her leg.

9 A tidy ghost.

10 A ghost that frightened the postman.

# Speaking and Listening

In groups, tell each other about spooky experiences that you and people in your family have had.

I never had a head for heights.

# Writing

Write one or two paragraphs for a magazine telling readers about one of your true experiences. You could write about a spooky experience, a time when you had a narrow escape, your most embarrassing moment or your most exciting experience.

On the right is what Penny wrote about her most embarrassing experience.

Earlier this year I went on a school Outward Bound holiday and I was sharing a room with three friends. When the teacher came round to wake us up one morning I was still half asleep. I thought I was at home being brought my morning cup of tea, so I called the teacher 'Mum'. I nearly died of embarrassment, but she thought it was really funny.

# Problems Pages

## ??? PROBLEMS PAGE ???

**If something is worrying you, don't bottle it up. Write to me and I'll do my best to help. Send your letters to Fiona, c/o _Teen-Scene_.**

Dear Fiona

You will probably think I haven't got much of a problem, but I feel my life is in ruins.

A few weeks ago I had a metal 'train track' brace fitted. It hurts, but what hurts more are the names that I'm called at school such as 'British Rail' and 'Mouthful'!

Please help me! I need your advice.

Tina

Dear Tina

Your mouth will soon get used to the brace, so it will stop hurting.

You will come to accept the look of the brace and you must remember why you are wearing it. It will be well worth it in the end, when you've got straight, even teeth and a perfect smile!

Show that the brace doesn't bother you and people will stop teasing you about it.

Best wishes

Fiona

Dear Fiona

I'm being bullied at school. The biggest boy in our year is making me give him money. He says if I don't give him £1 a week, he's going to beat me up. I'm scared that if I tell someone, he'll really lay into me.

Is there anything I can do?

Pete

Dear Pete

Bullies count on their victims keeping quiet. When you do have the courage to tell somebody and get help, the bullies lose their power.

The boy in your year is acting tough because he feels you are weaker than he is.

Tell a teacher you can trust, who will talk things through with you. Most schools have anti-bullying policies. I'm sure the bully and his friends will be dealt with.

Best wishes

Fiona

Dear Fiona

My mum's got a new boyfriend. He is good to us both, but I'm jealous of him being around all the time. He's not my real dad. He left us three years ago. Mum and I were OK on our own. I don't see why she should want to spend all her time with this stranger.

She might be happy, but I'm not!

Mitzy

Dear Mitzy

Your mum has probably been through a great deal in the past few years. You should be thrilled that she has found somebody new in her life.

Your turn will come soon and I'll bet your mum will support you when it does. She'll be happy to see you happy.

Best wishes

Fiona

# Speaking and Listening

In groups, read the letters on page 54 and Fiona's replies. Which of Fiona's replies do you think is:

- the most helpful;
- the least helpful?

On the right is another letter to Fiona. Put yourself in Fiona's position and discuss how you would reply to this letter.

Dear Fiona

Most of the time I get on well with my mum and dad. But now we've started to argue about what time I should come in at night.

I like to go out with my mates. We just hang about or go round someone's house to listen to CDs. We're not doing anything wrong, but my parents always want to know where I am and who I'm with.

It makes me feel like they don't trust me.

What can I do about it? It's really getting me down.

Marcus

Dear Fiona,
My problem is that I can never think what to write.

# Reading and Writing

Look at the problems pages in some teenage magazines. Find some letters that deal with the problems faced by 12- and 13-year-olds. Study the advice that is given and find at least one piece of advice that you agree with and one piece of advice that you disagree with.

Cut out the letters and replies and paste them on to a piece of paper. Write your own comments underneath, saying why you do or do not agree with the advice that is given.

# Writing

In groups, produce your own problems page.

Each think of a problem that someone of your age might write to a magazine about. Then draft the letter that the person might write.

Give your letter to someone else in the group. Then each draft a reply to the letter that you have been given.

Help each other to check the grammar, punctuation and spelling of the letters and the replies. Then stick them on a large sheet of paper and make a wall display of your problems pages.

# Topical Articles

Magazines often have articles about big events that are about to happen, such as a major concert or sporting event.

## Speaking and Listening

Read the article 'It's Carnival Time' (page 57).

Discuss what it tells you about:
- *where* the Carnival is held;
- *when* the Carnival is held;
- *what happens* at the Carnival.

List four things it tells you about steel bands.

## Writing

Below is the draft of a paragraph about the Wimbledon tennis championships. The writer forgot to punctuate it and has made several spelling mistakes. Copy it out neatly, putting in full stops and capital letters and correcting the spelling.

the bigest tennis event in britan is held at wimbledon it takes place at the end of june and begginning of july the tourniment is played on grass it is a long time since a british player won the mens signles the last british woman to win the womens signles was virginia wade

## Reading and Writing

**1** Choose an event that happens every year. It could be a sporting event such as the Grand National, the FA Cup Final or the British Grand Prix. It could be an annual show or a special day, such as Hallowe'en, Diwali or the Chinese New Year.

**2** Use the library and resources centre to find out about the event.

**3** Make notes about the event:
- List five key facts about the event, including *when* and *where* it takes place and *what happens;*
- List at least three interesting or unusual facts about the event.

**4** Use a computer and draft a short article about the event.

**5** Check the grammar, spelling and punctuation of your article, and then print out a copy.

# IT'S CARNIVAL TIME

The last week in August is carnival time and Notting Hill Carnival is one of the most famous. It is also fun! Monday is adult night and Sunday is children's night. Everyone wears colourful costumes. There are big feather hats and colourful dresses, shirts and trousers. All the colours of the rainbow are worn by the children. Proud mothers spend months making the costumes for the festival. The costumes are displayed during the procession through West London.

Everywhere steel bands play Afro-Caribbean music. The drums are often made from oil containers; the panels are beaten out with a hammer. Each dent in the top of the drum is carefully tuned to play a different note. This means that steel drums can play whole tunes, not just rhythms. There can be up to 100 drums in a band, but there are usually around 30. Together, the drums cover all the different voice types, although there are usually more deep bass drums than high soprano ones. Rubber-headed sticks are used to hit the drums.

# Your Own Magazine

In groups, design and write an eight-page magazine for people of your age. Use either a word processor or a **DTP** (desk-top publishing) program to design and produce your magazine.

## Stage 1:
### Planning the contents

- First, make a list of contents. On the right is the one Ramon's group made.
- Then decide who is going to design and write each page. Each person in the group should be responsible for at least one page.

Page 1 – Cover

Page 2 – Pop news and gossip

Page 3 – Readers' true experiences

Page 4 – Topical sports article

Page 5 – Problems page

Page 6 – Reviews of CDs and videos

Page 7 – Special report – Smoking

Page 8 – Horoscope

## Stage 2:
### Designing the pages

- Plan the layout of each page. Decide how you are going to divide the page into columns and how wide each column is going to be. You can use the DTP program to do this on the screen.

  It will show you a grid and you can plan where to put pictures as well as your writing. You also need to plan where you are going to put any headings and sub-headings.

- Choose a **typeface**. A typeface is the style in which you can print your text. Here are some samples of typefaces:

  This is Courier typeface.

  This is Helvetica typeface.

  This is Palatino typeface.

  This is New York typeface.

  The text can also be printed in different sizes. The size you choose will determine how many words you can fit into each column.

  Choose a style and size of typeface that is easy to read.

Some student magazines

# Stage 3: Drafting your text

Draft your writing on the screen.

When you have done your first draft, ask someone to look at it with you. Discuss how you could revise it in order to improve it by:

- adding or removing some sentences;
- changing the order of the sentences;
- changing some of the words.

# Stage 4: Checking

- Use the spellchecker to help you check for spelling errors. Then read the text to check for typing mistakes.
- Check that you have used full stops correctly and that you have left a space after each punctuation mark.
- Check that you have remembered to use paragraphs.
- Make sure that you have used capitals for the first letter of names of people and places.
- Check that the text fits into the spaces for it.
- Check that headings are in the right place.
- Check that any pictures or graphics fit the spaces for them.

When you have checked your page or pages, ask someone else to check it through before you print it.

# Stage 5:
## Publishing your magazine

Print out each of your pages and either bind them or staple them together to make your magazine. Print enough copies for each of the other groups to have a copy of your magazine.

# Speaking and Listening

When you have read each group's magazine, discuss them.

- Which magazine has the best range of contents?
- Which pages have the best layouts?
- Which pages are the most interesting to read?

Suggest any changes that might improve the magazines.

Decide which magazines are the best. Give your reasons.

**In this unit** you will be learning about how to develop arguments. You will be discussing your views on heroes and your ideal school, and writing letters expressing your opinions on local issues.

# Heroes

What makes someone a hero?

66 I admire the Spice Girls. They're a great act and I think they deserve everything they've achieved. 99

66 My hero is Nelson Mandela. He spent twenty-seven years in prison because he was prepared to stand up for the rights of black people. 99

66 People who are willing to risk their lives for other people – like *my* aunt. She's a fire officer and she rescued a baby from a burning house. 99

66 Sports stars like Alan Shearer are heroes. They've got lots of talent and they make the most of it. 99

66 People who put up with things and stay cheerful – like this girl I know who's in a wheelchair. 99

66 I think they are people with lots of courage, who *do* daring things, like sailing round the world on their own. 99

# Speaking and Listening

1 What do you think makes someone a hero?

2 On your own, write down the names of two famous people you admire and two ordinary people you admire. Think about why you admire them. Then, in groups, discuss your views and the views of the people on page 60.

3 Here is a list of qualities that someone suggested a hero must have:
   ● courage
   ● determination
   ● ambition
   ● talent
   ● unselfishness.

   Which of these qualities do you think is most important? Can you suggest any others?

# Man or Woman of the Century

1 Hold a class debate in which you choose the hero who you think should be named Man or Woman of the Century.

2 Work in pairs and prepare speeches to try to persuade the rest of the class to vote for the person you have chosen.

   ● As a whole class, do a brainstorm and make a list of candidates. Then, with the help of your teacher, choose the candidates and decide which person your pair is going to argue for.
   ● Use books and CD-ROMs to find out information about your candidate. Make notes about them under three headings: Life, Achievements, Personal Qualities.
   ● Draft your speech. You should give at least three reasons why you think the person should be named Man or Woman of the Century.
   ● Present your speeches. Then hold a vote to choose the Man or Woman of the Century. (Note: When you vote, you cannot vote for your own candidate!)

# The School I'd Like

I'd abolish school uniform. Everyone hates it and teachers waste a lot of time telling us off for not being in proper uniform. In my ideal school students would wear whatever they liked.

– Greg

First I would do something about the buildings. I'd get rid of all the temporary classrooms and replace them with new ones. I'd build a new sports hall with more modern equipment in it. Also I'd paint all the classrooms and put carpets in them.

– Hamid

There should be plants around the school, to make the place we work in look nicer. Teachers are always talking about the environment … ours could be much better!

– Marcus

There should be fewer school rules! There are so many at the moment that it is impossible to take them all in.

– Eleanor

Students should have more say in how the school is run. There should be a school council which would deal with students' complaints. Each class would elect two representatives to the council. They would suggest changes to the school rules.

– Salman

Some of the lessons are boring, so I'd make them more interesting. There would be lots more field trips to places of interest and there would be more talks, instead of having to learn everything from books.

– Janine

There should be a better counselling service for the bullied and for those that bully. A school anti-bullying policy means nothing without a proper follow-up.

– Sarah-Jane

I'd give every year group a common room, so that we don't get wet standing in the rain at break time. We could also sell food and drink to our year group and the profit could go to charity.

– Serena

# Speaking and Listening

**1** In groups, discuss the ideas expressed by the young people on page 62. Say whether you agree or disagree with each one, and give your reasons.

**2** What other changes would you like to make to your school, besides the ones that are suggested here?
Make a list of the changes you'd like to make under different headings:

- lessons
- homework
- school dinners
- rules
- uniform
- punishments
- school hours
- clubs and societies
- teachers.

What are the two changes that your group would most like to make? Discuss the reasons why you'd like to make those changes and choose someone to report your ideas to the rest of the class.

# Writing

Write about the changes you'd like to make at school to have 'The School I'd Like'. Make sure you give reasons for your suggestions in the way that the students on page 62 did.

*Classrooms should be redecorated and new furniture provided so that we can work in comfort.*

Remember to organise your writing in paragraphs. Each paragraph should be about the same idea or subject.

Before you start to write, make a paragraph plan like Jason's (on the right).

Remember to punctuate your paragraphs properly:

- Start the first sentence of each new paragraph on a new line.
- Leave a space between the margin and the first word of a new paragraph.

Paragraph 1 - Introduction - Why I want the changes

Paragraph 2 - Changes to buildings

Paragraph 3 - Abolish uniform

Paragraph 4 - Changes to lessons

Paragraph 5 - Introduce a school council

Paragraph 6 - Conclusion

# Letters to Newspapers

## Speaking and Listening

In groups, read and discuss these two letters, which were written to the local newspaper. Both of the writers give clear reasons for their views.

- What are Claire's reasons for wanting to keep her village library?
- What are Harriet's arguments for wanting floodlights at her tennis club?

**Dear Sir or Madam,**

I'm very upset about the decision to close my village library because of cuts in the Council budget. The library provides a great range of books which are used not just for pleasure but also to provide information for projects and school work. Many people in the village will no longer visit a library as the nearest one is almost 8 km away. Surely something as important as a library should be thought of as an essential service.

Yours faithfully, *Claire Jeffrey*

**Dear Sir or Madam,**

I am a keen tennis player and often play at my local club. It's very popular and the courts are always booked, even late at night. However, we can only play in the evening during summer when it stays light.

The club did apply for floodlights, but our request was refused. The Council said it would cause too much disturbance around the area. What the Council doesn't realise is that many local people would benefit. The club could stay open until 9.30 p.m. all year round, and the courts could be refurbished with the extra profit. Isn't it unfair to reduce the amount of tennis we could have?

Yours faithfully, *Harriet Slack*

## Writing

Write a letter to your local paper giving your views on a local issue. Either write about a real issue that is in the news, or imagine that your local swimming pool is going to be closed and write a letter arguing against the decision to close it. Make sure you give reasons for your views.

# Conjunctions

A **conjunction** is a joining word. The most common conjunction is the word <u>and</u>.

Conjunctions can join two words together, like fish <u>and</u> chips, wind <u>and</u> rain.

Other words that often act as conjunctions are:
*but, because, if, as, when, unless, so, until.*

A conjunction is often used to join two short sentences together to make one longer sentence.

Here is an example in which the conjunction <u>because</u> is used to join two sentences:
*Robin did not do his homework. He was out playing football.*
*Robin did not do his homework <u>because</u> he was out playing football.*

I woke up this morning,
<u>But</u> I had the conjunction blues,
<u>Because</u> my baby left me
<u>And</u> crept off with my shoes.
<u>If</u> you know where she's gone,
Please tell me all your news ...

## Exercise A

Join the two sentences to make one longer one by using one of these conjunctions:
*and, but, because, so.*

1 I scored a goal. I felt very pleased.
2 I cannot come out. I have to look after my baby brother.
3 She wanted to go on the trip. Her parents would not let her.
4 I was very angry. I slammed the door.
5 It started to rain. They put up their umbrellas.
6 We could not go to town. The car broke down.

## Exercise B

Use a conjunction to complete these sentences.

1 I am not allowed out ... I have tidied my room.
2 The dog started to bark ... he heard footsteps.
3 He fell over ... he did not hurt himself.
4 She cannot come at the moment ... she is on the telephone.
5 We will be champions ... we win tonight's match.
6 My mum was angry ... I was late home.

# The Oldtown By-pass

Here is an article from the *Oldtown Star* about a proposal to build a by-pass around Oldtown.

## GREEN LIGHT FOR NEW BY-PASS

The Department of Transport has announced plans for a by-pass to be built round Oldtown. The road will be a dual carriageway and will go to the north of Oldtown. It will run from the Piper's Cross superstore at the west end of the town to the Hawksford Road roundabout at the north-east of the town.

The decision was greeted with relief by Councillor Jane Johnson, the leader of Oldtown Council. 'We've waited too long for a by-pass. Anyone who tries to get through Oldtown in the rush hour knows just how much the by-pass is needed.'

However, not everyone is happy with the decision. The route of the new by-pass takes it through farm-land and land belonging to the Oldtown Golf Club. A meeting organised by the Stop the By-Pass action group is to be held in St Mary's Hall on Wednesday 10 March at 7.30 p.m.

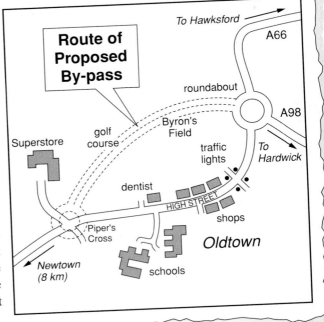

## What People Think About the By-pass

These comments were made during a radio phone-in programme about the by-pass.

'The by-pass is an excellent idea. As a mother of two small children, I won't have to worry any more about lorries rumbling through the High Street. There have been two accidents in the past six months.'
– *Mrs Shirley Biggs (mother)*

'It's a disgraceful idea. The golf course will lose its practice ground and it will destroy Byron's Field and valuable farm-land.'
– *Major Franklin-Smythe (Oldtown Golf Club)*

'It's a mixed blessing. People will be able to get into Oldtown more easily, but they won't have to come. I expect we'll lose even more trade to out-of-town superstores like the one at Piper's Cross.'
– *Ivan Wiltshire (shopkeeper)*

'At long last. I'm fed up of being stuck in traffic jams crawling through Oldtown High Street. It will cut my journey to work by half an hour.'
– *Sunil Prasad (motorist)*

'We need to think of ways of cutting down car use and reducing pollution rather than simply building more and more new roads.'
– *Eva Burton (Save the Countryside campaigner)*

**Left:** *A petition organised by Farmers and Friends Against the By-Pass.*

**Below:** *Oldtown High Street.*

### Farmers and Friends Against the By-Pass

The Oldtown by-pass will destroy valuable farm-land and damage the countryside.

*SAVE THE BADGER*

The new road will destroy the homes of several families of badgers. There is a badger run between the golf course and Byron's Field. Badgers will be killed by speeding traffic.

*PROTECT THE COUNTRYSIDE*

Large areas of farm-land will be lost. Wild flowers will be destroyed. Some species may be lost forever.

Building a by-pass is not necessary. We can find other ways of solving Oldtown's traffic problems, such as car-sharing schemes and better public transport.

Help us to save the countryside by signing below.

I am totally opposed to the proposal to build the Oldtown By-Pass.

| Signature | Name and Address (Please Print) |
| --- | --- |
|  |  |
|  |  |
|  |  |
|  |  |
|  |  |

# Speaking and Listening

1 In pairs, discuss the proposal to build the Oldtown by-pass. Make lists of:
   - the reasons why some people are *for* the by-pass;
   - the reasons why some people are *against* the by-pass.

2 In groups of three, role-play a scene in which a TV interviewer talks to two people with different views. One of them is for the by-pass. The other is against the by-pass.

3 As a class, role-play a public meeting in which people argue for and against the new by-pass.

# Writing

Write a letter to the local paper, the *Oldtown Star.* Give your reasons why you are for or against the by-pass.

# The Comma

A **comma** looks like this **,** and has several uses. It is used to break up lists of words and to separate the different parts of long sentences. The comma is a very common punctuation mark, but it is one of the hardest to use correctly.

Commas are used to separate the words in a list. Here are some examples:
*Remember to pack your socks, shorts, T-shirts, swimming costume and a towel.*
*For breakfast I had sausage, bacon, egg, tomato and fried bread.*

Notice that you do not have to use a comma after the last but one item on the list, when it is joined to the final item by 'and'.

> We have egg and chips egg and ham ham and chips egg ham and chips sausage and egg sausage egg and chips but sausage and chips are off sorry.

Commas are also used to separate phrases. (Note: A **phrase** is a group of words that only makes full sense as part of a sentence.) For example:
*I like riding my bicycle, playing football, listening to CDs and watching videos.*

## Exercise A

Each of these sentences contains a list. Copy them out and put in commas to mark off the separate items.

1 She was wearing a cap T-shirt jeans and trainers.
2 At the shop he bought a sandwich a drink a magazine and a newspaper.
3 Manchester United Arsenal Tottenham Hotspur Liverpool and Birmingham City have all won the FA Cup.
4 We have maths history geography and science homework tonight.
5 I am meeting Naseem Jason Susan and Winston after school.
6 The train stopped at Crewe Stafford Wolverhampton Birmingham and Coventry.
7 We visited the zoo the castle the museum and the park.
8 In her pencil case she had a pencil a rubber a ruler and a biro.

## Exercise B

Each of these sentences contains a list of phrases. Copy them out and put in commas to mark off the separate phrases.

1 I've looked on the mantelpiece on the window sills under the cushions and behind the sofa.
2 We have learned how to make a sling how to put on a bandage how to stop bleeding and how to make a splint.
3 You go down the street across the square up some steps and into the market.
4 He is good at heading the ball trapping it dribbling round defenders and shooting at goal.
5 Before you go out you must do the dishes tidy your room empty your wastepaper basket and put your washing out.

Commas are also used to show where there is a break or pause in a long sentence. You often use a comma when two parts of a sentence are joined by a conjunction, such as 'and', 'but' or 'because'. For example:

*I wanted to come out last night and play football with you, but my mum made me stay in and finish my homework.*

# Exercise C

Each of these long sentences has been joined by using a conjunction. Copy them out and put commas in each of them to show where there is a pause in the sentence.

1 Terry will be off school next week because he has to go into hospital for an operation on his leg.

2 There was a very long queue at the bus stop so I had to wait for over half an hour for a bus.

3 I wanted to buy a new skirt but they did not have one in the right colour.

4 It seemed certain that she would win the race until she fell over going round the last bend.

5 My mum says that we're going on holiday to Florida and I am really looking forward to it.

6 I don't think I'm going to pass the exam unless I do a lot more work than I'm doing at present.

# Exercise D

It can sometimes be hard to decide whether to use a full stop or a comma. Each of the following statements is either a single sentence containing a comma, or two short sentences separated by a full stop. The asterisk (*) tells you where a comma or full stop should be. Copy out each of the statements, putting in either a comma or a full stop. Remember, if it is a full stop you must put a capital letter at the beginning of the word that comes after it.

1 Sita is one of our best players * she has scored more goals than anyone else.

2 My uncle has developed a bad cough * because he smokes too many cigarettes.

3 We couldn't find the rest of the group * so we went back to the starting point.

4 The book I am reading is very good * it tells the story of a young disabled girl.

5 I do not think England will win the World Cup * they haven't got enough world-class players.

6 We waited at the stage door for nearly an hour * but we didn't get their autographs.

7 The spaceship was badly damaged * the astronauts had to change their plans.

8 The shopkeeper said he would change it * if I showed him the receipt.

**In this unit** you will be reading stories about a U.F.O. and a space adventure. You will be learning about how to write descriptions and writing your own story about a U.F.O.

# The U.F.O.

## The U.F.O.

Paul Trent and his wife lived on a farm in Oregon in the USA. On 11 May 1950 at about 7.45 p.m. they claim that they saw a U.F.O. Mr Trent took two photographs of it. The photographs have never been proved to be fakes.

It was a cool, clear, dry evening. Mrs Trent was on the south side of the house feeding the rabbits. She looked up and saw a disc-shaped object to the north-east. The object was moving westwards.

She called to Mr Trent, who was inside the house. When he saw how unusual the object looked, Mr Trent ran to his car to fetch his camera. But Mrs Trent remembered that he had left it in the house, so she hurried in to fetch it.

The object was tilted up a little as it approached and looked bright and silvery. It made no noise, and Mr and Mrs Trent saw no smoke or vapour.

Mr Trent took a picture and wound on ready for the next frame. He moved to the right to keep the object in the viewfinder and took a second shot about thirty seconds after the first.

Mrs Trent said the object seemed to be gliding. They felt a breeze as the object tilted before flying overhead. Mr Trent estimated its diameter as around 6 to 9 metres. The object moved off to the west and then 'dimly vanished'.

# Reading and Writing

Read the story of 'The U.F.O.' (page 70). Then answer these questions by copying out the sentences and choosing the correct answer from the three answers given in the brackets.

1 Mr and Mrs Trent lived on a farm in
   (*a* Scotland *b* America *c* Australia).

2 They saw the U.F.O. on 11 May 1950 in
   (*a* the morning *b* the afternoon
   *c* the evening).

3 The weather that day was
   (*a* hot and sticky *b* cool and dry
   *c* cold and wet).

4 When Mrs Trent saw the U.F.O. she was
   (*a* watering the garden
   *b* feeding the rabbits
   *c* feeding the chickens).

5 The object was shaped like
   (*a* a disc *b* a cigar *c* an umbrella).

6 When the object appeared,
   Mr Trent was
   (*a* in the barn *b* in the garage
   *c* in the house).

7 Mrs Trent fetched her husband's
   camera from
   (*a* the car *b* the caravan
   *c* the house).

8 Mr Trent took
   (*a* two pictures *b* four pictures
   *c* six pictures).

9 The object was
   (*a* dull and black
   *b* bright and silvery
   *c* shiny and golden).

10 As it passed overhead, the object made
   (*a* a roaring sound
   *b* a hissing sound
   *c* no sound).

11 As it moved, the object seemed to be
   (*a* spinning *b* rocking from side
   to side *c* gliding).

12 The object moved off and vanished
   (*a* to the north *b* to the west
   *c* to the south).

# Speaking and Listening

In groups of three, role-play a scene in which a TV or radio reporter interviews Mr and Mrs Trent and asks them about what they saw. Before you begin, draw up a list of questions for the reporter to ask Mr and Mrs Trent. Here is the start of such a list:

● What time of day was it when you saw the object?

● What were you doing at the time it appeared?

● What made you think it was a U.F.O.?

# Writing

Write a report for the local newspaper about the sighting of the U.F.O. Make sure you write in paragraphs and that your report contains all the most important details about the sighting.

A good newspaper report will give you information that answers these questions:
● What happened?
● Who did it happen to?
● Where did it happen?
● When did it happen?
● Why did it happen?

# Mission to Zeda

It is the year 3001. Planet Earth faces a crisis. The Earth is suffering from global warming. Food and water are running short. The only hope seems to be to find new planets that could support human life.

Captain Swithin and his crew have been sent to explore Planet Zeda.

The extract on the right is from Captain Swithin's log-book, describing what he saw when they landed.

We have landed on Planet Zeda. The sky is deep blue, not a cloud in sight! The planet is very cold and my hands are frozen. This must be Zeda's winter, or maybe it is always cold here.

Outside everything is white. The whole planet appears to be covered in deep snow. Growing through the snow are pink jelly-like plants that blow gently in the light breeze. It looks as if the plants are dancing. One of the crew has given them a name – the 'pink drifts'.

On the horizon are tall, thin, grey mountains. With snow all around them they look like abandoned fairy castles.

There are dark trees near the foot of the mountains and plants with blue flowers. The blue flowers twist around the tree trunks like ivy. Round golden balls hang from the trees like Christmas decorations. We think they must be fruit, as they look like they might be good to eat. But I've warned the crew not to touch them until we have examined them more closely.

## Speaking and Listening

1 On your own, list five facts that you learn about Zeda from this entry in Captain Swithin's log. Then, in groups, compare your lists.

2 Suggest names that the crew might give to:
  ● the mountains
  ● the trees
  ● the plants with blue flowers.

3 Study the picture of Zeda (page 73). Pick out all the things Captain Swithin describes. Then discuss what else you can see in the picture.

## Writing

Imagine you are Captain Swithin. Write one or two more paragraphs, describing the other things you can see in the picture.

# Speaking and Listening

On the right is another entry from Captain Swithin's log-book, three days later.

- In groups, discuss what you learn about the Ice Orcs from this entry.
- Imagine that Captain Swithin and his crew are captured and taken to the Ice Orcs' underground city. Discuss what you think the Ice Orcs' city would be like. Make notes of your ideas. Choose someone to act as your reporter and share your ideas in a class discussion.

Today, we travelled towards the mountains but had to turn back before we reached them. We met strange alien creatures. The crew have named them Ice Orcs. They live underground and come out to hunt. When they are hunting, they march in two long lines.

The creatures are small with monkey-like faces and furry bodies. They carry spears that gleam in the sun. The spears are as long as their bodies and they look like ice. They have surrounded the spacecraft.

I have called a meeting of the crew. There is nothing we can do, except to surrender.

# Writing

Imagine that Captain Swithin and his crew make friends with some of the Ice Orcs. The friendly Ice Orcs help them to plan their escape. The map (page 75) shows the route the crew has to take and the dangers they must face.

Write four entries from Captain Swithin's log, describing their escape.

- **Entry 1**. Describe how the friendly Ice Orcs helped the crew to escape from the prison. How did they get past the guards without being seen? Describe the Ice Orcs' city and how the crew were chased along the road until they reached the entrance of the secret tunnel.

- **Entry 2**. Describe the journey through the secret tunnel. Explain what it was like in the tunnel and what they saw when they came to the Pit of Spikes. How did the friendly Ice Orcs help them to get safely round the Pit of Spikes?
- **Entry 3**. Describe what they saw when they came to the Frozen Lake and the cave of Miron the Lake Monster. Explain what happened when Miron smelt them, as they tried to creep by.
- **Entry 4**. Describe the final part of their journey as they crossed the Ice Mountains. Write about the difficulty they had finding a path to the top. Describe the view from the top and how they felt when they saw the spaceship.

# Speaking and Listening

Imagine that on his return to Earth, Captain Swithin held a press conference. He answered questions about Zeda and about how they were imprisoned and escaped. Choose someone to be hot-seated as Captain Swithin and role-play the press conference, with everyone else taking the part of reporters.

# Writing

Write your own story about a U.F.O. landing in a park where you were playing. Plan your story in paragraphs.

● **Paragraph 1**. Describe the park where you were playing. Say what time it was and what the weather was like.

● **Paragraph 2**. Describe the U.F.O. appearing and landing.

● **Paragraph 3**. Describe how the U.F.O. opened and what the aliens looked like.

● **Paragraph 4**. Describe what the aliens did.

● **Paragraph 5**. Describe how the aliens returned to the U.F.O. and how it took off and disappeared.

# Punctuation Practice – Apostrophes

The **apostrophe** is shaped like a comma, but it is written above the line, like this ' and has two main uses.

It is used to show where a letter or letters have been missed out of a word (see *English Direct*, Book 1, page 49).

It is also used to show *possession* or *ownership*.

'The dog of Paul has taken the ball of Claire.'

## Apostrophes of Possession

We use apostrophes to make it easier to say that something belongs to someone.

For example, 'Mum's car' is shorter and easier to say than 'the car of Mum' or 'the car belonging to Mum'.

There are three main rules about how to use apostrophes of possession.

## Rule 1

When the word is *singular* (meaning there is only one owner) you add '<u>s</u> (apostrophe + s). For example:
the <u>cat's</u> tail, the <u>man's</u> hat, <u>Sam's</u> bag.

Copy out the following phrases and make them shorter and easier to say by using apostrophes.

1 The jacket of my brother.
2 The whistle of the referee.
3 The basket of the dog.
4 The pencil of Robin.
5 The helmet of the cyclist.

## Rule 2

When the word is *plural* (meaning there is more than one owner) and the word ends in <u>s</u> you add ' (apostrophe). For example:
the <u>boys'</u> changing-room, my <u>parents'</u> flat.

Copy out the following phrases and make them shorter and easier to say by using apostrophes.

1 The staffroom of the teachers.
2 The desks of the students.
3 The boots of the footballers.
4 The barking of the dogs.
5 The guns of the soldiers.

# Rule 3

When the word is *plural* but does not end in
<u>s</u> you add <u>'s</u> (apostrophe + s). For example:
*the <u>children's</u> voices, the <u>men's</u> photographs.*

Copy out the following phrases and make them
shorter and easier to say by using apostrophes.

1 The shouts of the people.

2 The faces of the women.

3 The books of the children.

4 The shirts of the men.

Learn this rhyme to help you to
remember how to use the
apostrophe.

There is just one owner.
No need to guess,
Just add apostrophe s!

There are lots of owners.
Then you can see,
You only need an apostrophe.

# Writing

Here is part of an adventure story
that Hamid wrote. He forgot to use
any apostrophes. Copy it out and
put in the apostrophes.

Jackson came to the caves
mouth. He switched on the
torchs beam. Jackson's heart
was beating fast. The beam
lit up the caves slimy walls.
The giant bats wings
brushed his face as they
swooped around him. He
could hear the monsters
growls as it sharpened its
claws. He listened again but
could not hear his friends
voices. Jacksons face twisted
into a smile. Once again he
had to go it alone.

# The Pardoner's Tale

This story comes from *The Canterbury Tales*, one of the most famous pieces of writing in English. It was written in about 1380 by Geoffrey Chaucer. The tale is one of the stories told by a group of people, known as pilgrims, on a journey from London to Canterbury. The pilgrims were going to visit the tomb of Thomas Becket, a priest who was murdered in Canterbury Cathedral. They took it in turns to tell each other stories.

In those days the Church was much more powerful than it is today. The Pardoner was a church official who sold people pardons for their sins, so that they would go to heaven.

His tale is about three drunkards who go looking for Death.

## The Pardoner's Tale

There were these three drunkards. They were angry because Death had just killed their friend. They decided to go looking for him.

'We'll sort him out,' they said. 'The innkeeper told us he killed everyone in that village where they had the plague. He can't be far away.'

A few hundred yards down the road, they met an old man. The old man spoke to them politely, but they were rude to him and accused him of being a spy for Death. They demanded to know where Death was.

'Follow this crooked path towards the wood,' said the old man. 'You'll find him waiting near the oak tree.'

The three men hurried along the path, but there was no one waiting for them by the tree. Instead, they found a huge pile of gold coins.

At once they forgot all about Death. 'We're rich,' they cried. 'It's true that Fortune has favoured us,' said the wickedest one. 'But we've got to be careful. If we just turn up loaded with gold, everyone will think we're robbers. We'll have to take it back at night. Meanwhile, one of us should go back and buy us some bread and wine from the town. The other two will stay here and guard the treasure.'

So they drew lots and the youngest drew the shortest straw. He set off for the town to buy bread and wine.

As soon as he was gone, one of the wicked men turned and said to the other one: 'If the two of us share the gold, there'll be more for us than if the three of us share it. Let's kill him when he gets back.' So they made a plan to stab him in the back when he returned.

Meanwhile, as he neared town, the youngest one was thinking: 'Why don't I get rid of those two old fools and keep all the money for myself?'

He decided that he would poison them. So he found a chemist and pretended that he needed some poison to protect his chickens from rats and from a polecat. He bought a powerful poison that the chemist said would kill any creature that drank it. Then he bought some bottles of wine and put the poison in two of them.

When the youngest one got back to his friends, they jumped on him and murdered him, just as they had planned. After killing him, they opened a bottle of wine to celebrate. It was one of the poisoned bottles. One of them took a swig, then passed it to the other one. Within an instant, they were both dead.

That is how the three men met Death.

# Speaking and Listening

In groups, act out 'The Pardoner's Tale' as a series of scenes:

- *Scene 1: In the inn.* The three men tell the innkeeper they are going to find Death and sort him out.
- *Scene 2: On the road.* The three men meet the old man.
- *Scene 3: At the oak tree.* They find the gold and discuss what to do.
- *Scene 4: At the oak tree.* The two men plot to kill the younger man.
- *Scene 5: At the chemist's.* The youngest man buys the poison.
- *Scene 6: At the oak tree.* The three men die.

Take it in turns to present your role-plays to the rest of the class. Discuss which of your scenes worked the best and why.

# Writing

In pairs, re-tell 'The Pardoner's Tale' as a picture-strip. Discuss how many pictures you will need and how many pages you will need for your pictures. Then draw your picture-strip and write captions and speech-bubbles. Do not worry if you are not very good at drawing. Stick people will do!

# The Development of the English Language

When Chaucer wrote *The Canterbury Tales*, the English language looked and sounded very different from the language we speak and write today. Chaucer used a form of the language known as **Middle English** from which Modern English later developed. Many of the words Chaucer used were different from the words we use today, and many words were spelt differently.

On the right is part of 'The Pardoner's Tale' as Chaucer wrote it; beneath it is a modern translation.

*And with that word it happed hym, par cas,*
*To take the botel ther the poysoun was,*
*And drank and yaf his felawe drynke also*
*For which anon they storven bothe two.*

And with those words it happened, by chance,

that he took the bottle with the poison in it,

and he drank and gave his friend a drink also,

which is why they both died instantly.

## Reading and Writing

A good dictionary will tell you the *origin* of words as well as their *meaning*. On the right are two entries from the *Collins School Dictionary*. The information in square brackets at the end of each entry tells you where the word has come from.

The words in the list below came into the English language from different sources. Some of them are **Old English** words. Others came from **Old Norse**, **Latin** and French.

1 Put the words in alphabetical order.
2 Use a dictionary to find out which came from Old English, which from Old Norse, which from Latin and which from French.

garage  window  bottle  medical  skirt  ugly
crowd  nostril  home  punish  trumpet  restaurant

**gate, gates**
(noun) A gate is a barrier which can open and shut and is used to close the entrance to a garden or field. [from Old Norse *gat* meaning 'opening' or 'passage']

**brunette, brunettes**
(noun) A brunette is a girl or woman with dark brown hair. [from French *brunet* meaning 'dark' or 'brownish']

# Speaking and Listening

Study the map below, which tells you about how the English language developed. What do you learn from it about the different sources that English words have come from?

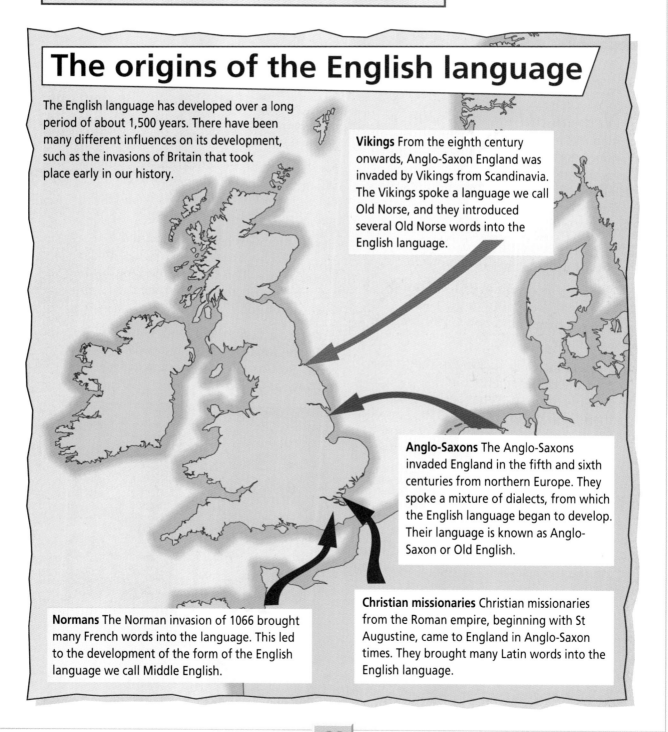

# The origins of the English language

The English language has developed over a long period of about 1,500 years. There have been many different influences on its development, such as the invasions of Britain that took place early in our history.

**Vikings** From the eighth century onwards, Anglo-Saxon England was invaded by Vikings from Scandinavia. The Vikings spoke a language we call Old Norse, and they introduced several Old Norse words into the English language.

**Anglo-Saxons** The Anglo-Saxons invaded England in the fifth and sixth centuries from northern Europe. They spoke a mixture of dialects, from which the English language began to develop. Their language is known as Anglo-Saxon or Old English.

**Normans** The Norman invasion of 1066 brought many French words into the language. This led to the development of the form of the English language we call Middle English.

**Christian missionaries** Christian missionaries from the Roman empire, beginning with St Augustine, came to England in Anglo-Saxon times. They brought many Latin words into the English language.

# How Ganesh Became Rich and Famous – An Indian Story

*Near an old woman's hut,* a man-eating tiger was sheltering from the rain. Inside the hut, the old woman was grumbling about the storm. 'What a terrible downpour!' she said. 'It's more fierce than any tiger.'

The tiger heard what she said. It wondered who this 'terrible downpour' was. It must be someone very fierce.

Just then a poor man called Ganesh came staggering down the road. He was drunk and he was looking for his donkey.

He saw the tiger lurking in the shadow near the old woman's hut. He thought it was his donkey. 'What are you doing there, you miserable beast?' he shouted. He grabbed the tiger by the ear and started to beat it with a stick.

The tiger was so frightened that it just stood there. It thought Ganesh must be the 'terrible downpour' that the old woman had talked about.

Ganesh threw down the stick and leapt on the tiger's back. He rode it down the road to his house. When he got home, he tied it to a post. He staggered into the house and immediately fell fast asleep.

Next morning, when his wife went outside, she was amazed to find the tiger tied to the post. She ran indoors to wake up Ganesh and ask him about it. He had no idea how the tiger had got there.

News of the tiger spread through the village. When the villagers asked Ganesh how he had caught it, Ganesh just shrugged his shoulders.

Stories that Ganesh had captured a tiger with his bare hands reached the royal palace. The ruler of the kingdom, the mighty Rajah, came to see the captured tiger.

'You are a very brave man, Ganesh,' said the Rajah. 'My army needs men like you.' So Ganesh was made a Lord and a General.

*Soon afterwards,* a neighbouring ruler was preparing to attack the kingdom. All the other generals in the Rajah's army refused to fight. So the Rajah made Ganesh the Commander-in-Chief of his horsemen.

Ganesh had never ridden a horse. But he thanked the Rajah and went to look for a quiet pony for himself. However, the Rajah sent him a magnificent stallion.

'What am I going to do?' he asked his wife.

'Leave it to me,' she said. 'I've got an idea.'

She helped Ganesh to climb on the massive horse. Then she tied his legs together with a strap underneath the horse's stomach.

'Off you go,' she said and gave the horse a slap. At once it galloped off, with Ganesh clinging to its mane.

Soon Ganesh realised that he was heading towards the enemy's camp. This terrified him so much that he decided to grab at a big banyan tree to make himself stop. But he was travelling so fast that the tree was uprooted from the ground into his arms. Instead of stopping him, it made him roar with pain.

The enemy look-outs saw the enormous horse and what looked like a huge man on its back. Rumours spread through the enemy camp that a mighty army of men was coming towards them. The men were so fierce that they tore up trees in their rage.

Soon the whole of the enemy army was in a state of panic. They made their leaders write a peace treaty and fled as fast as they could.

When Ganesh reached the camp, the strap holding him onto the horse broke from the strain. Ganesh fell off the horse. But the camp was empty. Nobody was there to see him as he moaned about his aches and pains and limped among the tents. He found the peace treaty and all the riches that the enemy had left behind.

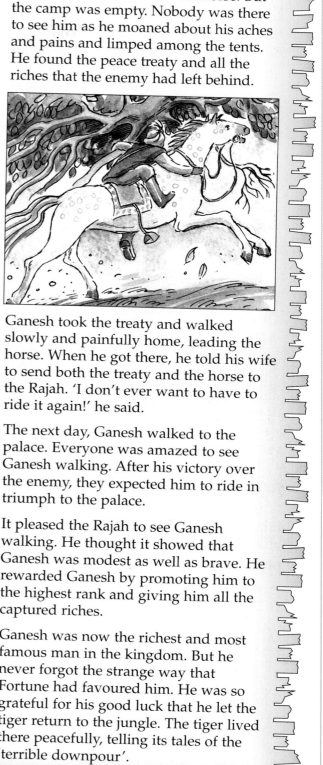

Ganesh took the treaty and walked slowly and painfully home, leading the horse. When he got there, he told his wife to send both the treaty and the horse to the Rajah. 'I don't ever want to have to ride it again!' he said.

The next day, Ganesh walked to the palace. Everyone was amazed to see Ganesh walking. After his victory over the enemy, they expected him to ride in triumph to the palace.

It pleased the Rajah to see Ganesh walking. He thought it showed that Ganesh was modest as well as brave. He rewarded Ganesh by promoting him to the highest rank and giving him all the captured riches.

Ganesh was now the richest and most famous man in the kingdom. But he never forgot the strange way that Fortune had favoured him. He was so grateful for his good luck that he let the tiger return to the jungle. The tiger lived there peacefully, telling its tales of the 'terrible downpour'.

# Reading and Writing

Read the story 'How Ganesh Became Rich and Famous' (pages 82–83), then write sentences in answer to these questions.

1 What did the tiger think when he heard the old woman complaining about the rain?

2 Why did Ganesh grab the tiger by the ear and start beating it?

3 Why didn't the tiger attack Ganesh?

4 Why didn't Ganesh tell the villagers how he had captured the tiger?

5 Why did the Rajah make Ganesh one of his generals?

6 How did Ganesh feel when the Rajah gave him a magnificent horse?

7 How did Ganesh's wife help him to ride the horse?

8 How did Ganesh try to stop the horse when it was charging towards the enemy camp?

9 Why did the enemy run away?

10 What did Ganesh find in the enemy camp?

11 Why were the people surprised to see Ganesh walking to the palace?

12 What did the Rajah think when he saw Ganesh walking to the palace?

13 What reward did the Rajah give Ganesh?

14 Why did Ganesh set the tiger free?

# The Plot

Remember that every story has a **plot**. The plot of a story is the outline of the series of events that happen in the story. Often the plot of a story can be shown in a flow-chart.

Draw a flow-chart to show the plot of 'How Ganesh Became Rich and Famous'. Here is the start of such a flow-chart.

A man-eating tiger hears an old woman talking about a fierce creature.

A poor man called Ganesh looks drunkenly for his donkey.

# Speaking and Listening

The **moral** of a story is the message that the story gives to the reader. In groups, discuss which of these statements best sums up the moral of the story about Ganesh.

1 People who take risks will end up rich.

2 A poor man needs good luck if he's going to become rich.

3 You do not have to be clever to be brave.

4 A ruler will always reward a brave man.

# Adverbs

An **adverb** is a word that adds information about part of the sentence, usually the verb. For example, an adverb tells *how*, *when* or *where* something is done. 'Slowly', 'now' and 'here' are all adverbs.

In many sentences an adverb is placed immediately after the verb. For example:
> The teacher shouted <u>angrily</u>.
> The girl laughed <u>loudly</u>.

Many adverbs end in <u>-ly</u> and are formed by adding <u>-ly</u> to an adjective. For example:
> sad + <u>ly</u> = sadly
> calm + <u>ly</u> = calmly.

**Verbs** tell of something being done;
To <u>read</u>, <u>count</u>, <u>sing</u>, <u>laugh</u>, <u>jump</u> or <u>run</u>.
How things are done the **adverbs** tell –
<u>Slowly</u>, <u>quickly</u>, <u>badly</u> or <u>well</u>.

## Writing

Copy out these sentences and complete them by choosing a suitable adverb from the list on the right.

| | |
|---|---|
| awkwardly | slowly |
| cheerfully | fiercely |
| viciously | loudly |
| silently | quickly |
| happily | nervously |

1 The crowd cheered … when a goal was scored.
2 Yasmin ran … down the road to the bus-stop.
3 My baby sister smiled … as she opened her presents.
4 The tiger paced up and down and growled …
5 Tony whistled … because he was in a good mood.
6 Tina waited … outside the Head's study.
7 He limped … down the steps of the hospital.
8 The robber moved … across the grass towards the house.
9 The guard dog snarled … and bared its teeth.
10 She fell … and broke her arm.

# American Slavery

## JOSHUA

Let me tell you about Joshua. He arrived on the plantation one day when I was about seven. Where he came from nobody knew. He never spoke about his past.

They called him Joshua Parsons. Parsons wasn't his real name. Slaves took on the surnames of their owners. Their real names were lost.

We knew right away that Joshua was different. He arrived on a cart. One of his eyes was closed up and there was blood trickling from a gash at the corner of his mouth. It was obvious that he had been beaten for some reason. There were lots of rumours about what he'd done, but no one knew for sure.

At first, people kept away from Joshua. They were frightened that if they were friendly to him the overseers would pick on them. That was the way it was on the plantations.

But my mammy wasn't afraid. She took him in, bathed his wounds and he found himself a place to sleep in the corner of our cabin.

Joshua was strong and tough. During the day the overseers kept a close eye on him as he worked in the fields. But he kept his head down and kept out of trouble.

At night-times, though, Joshua and my mammy would talk. But it was dangerous talk. Joshua would talk about how wrong it all was.

He'd talk about the rights of black people, how black and white were born equal, and how sinful it was of people like Thomas Parsons to keep black people as slaves. He said we must learn to read and write. Then we'd be able to stand up for our rights.

Mammy laughed when he said that. There weren't any schools on the plantations. How could slave children learn to read and write?

There was a way, he said. If mammy would let him, he'd teach me. I begged mammy to let him. But she was scared. If I was caught, they'd whip me. I'd bear the scars for ever – scars like the ones on Joshua's back.

But Joshua never got the chance to teach me. They came for him early one morning and dragged him out of the cabin. They forced him into a cart and drove him off to town. We heard later that he'd been sold.

Joshua never came back. What happened to him, I do not know. But I never forgot what Joshua had said. So I made a vow – a vow that one day I'd learn to read and write, and that I'd do what Joshua said we must do and speak up for our rights.

*James Rigg*

## Speaking and Listening

In groups, read the story about Joshua, then discuss these questions:

- Who is telling the story of Joshua? Why does he or she remember Joshua?
- Make a list of everything you learn about Joshua in the story. What impression of Joshua does the story give?
- What do you learn from the story about life on a plantation and about the way slaves were treated?

## Reading

Read *Nightjohn* by Gary Paulsen (Pan). It tells the story of a slave who risked everything in order to teach young black slaves how to read and write.

This poem was written in 1852. It was part of a speech made by a black American woman called Sojourner Truth at a women's rights meeting. At that time, black American women had no rights.

# Ain't I a Woman?

That man over there say
a woman needs to be helped
  into carriages
and lifted over ditches
and to have the best place
  everywhere.
Nobody ever helped me into
  carriages
or over mud puddles
or gives me a best place ...
and ain't I a woman?

Look at me.
Look at my arm!
I have plowed and planted
and gathered into barns
and no man could head me ...
and ain't I a woman?

I could work as much
and eat as much as a man —
when I could get it —
and bear the lash as well ...
and ain't I a woman?

I have borne thirteen children
and seen most all sold into slavery
and when I cried out a
  mother's grief
none but Jesus heard me ...
and ain't I a woman?

Sojourner Truth (1797–1883)

## Speaking and Listening

In groups, read the poem and discuss these questions.

- What arguments does Sojourner Truth present in order to support her view that women should have the same rights as men?
- Do you think she presents a strong case? Give your reasons.
- Talk about what you learn about Sojourner Truth and her life from this poem.

Now take it in turns to read the poem aloud to the rest of the group. Try to put lots of expression into your reading. Decide whose reading puts her arguments across most powerfully, and get that person to perform their reading to the rest of the class.

## In Pairs

One of you is a newspaper reporter, the other an anti-slavery campaigner who has seen a child taken from its mother and sold as a slave. Role-play the scene in which the newspaper reporter interviews the campaigner.

## Research and Writing

Use the resources centre to find out about the conditions in which slaves lived on plantations in the southern states of America during the early nineteenth century. Make notes, and then use your notes to help you to write either a short article about what it was like to be a slave, or some entries for the diary of a slave.

**In this unit** you will be reading a scene from a play and staging a performance of it. You will learn who does what in the theatre, and you will also be writing and performing some short plays of your own.

# Rule Four: Keep Clear of Pringle

*The scene is a boarding school dormitory. At first, only Nicky can be seen, standing stage left.*

**Pringle:** *(shouting, backstage)* Quadir!

**Nicky:** *(addressing the audience)* And Rule Four: Keep clear of Pringle.

**Pringle:** *(more loudly, still backstage)* Quadir!

*Nicky walks stage right and, as the right-hand side of the stage is lit up, we see that there's now an iron bed and two chairs. Quadir, an owlish Asian boy, is reading a book on the bed. Another boy, Paul, is sitting on a chair, playing a mini-computer game. Both are about Nicky's age.*

**Nicky:** *(still to the audience)* My dorm. That's Paul. And this is Quadir – like a death wish on legs.

*Pringle, an older boy with angry spots, bursts in. He's carrying a pair of shoes. Nicky sits on the other chair.*

**Pringle:** Are you deaf, Ali Baba?

**Quadir:** *(with dignity)* The name's Quadir.

**Pringle:** *(throwing the shoes on the floor by the bed)* Clean them, boy.

**Quadir:** My parents told me there was no fagging at Holton.

**Pringle:** Your parents? I don't see any parents round here.

**Quadir:** They said –

**Pringle:** If those shoes aren't shining in two minutes, I'll just have to do your face some serious harm. Comprende? *(He storms out. Quadir goes back to reading his book. There's an awkward silence.)*

**Paul:** Quadir.

**Quadir:** *(as if nothing has happened)* Hmm?

**Nicky:** Just do it, Quadir.

**Quadir:** My parents were definitely told that there was no fagging.

**Nicky:** Don't you understand? The guy's a psycho. He won't just make *your* life hell – it'll be all of us. It doesn't matter what anyone tells your parents. This is just between Pringle and us.

**Quadir:** It's the principle that counts. *(Paul angrily picks up the shoes and begins to polish them.)* I'll ring my parents.

**Nicky:** Don't. Anyway we're not allowed to ring home for the first three weeks. You know that. *(As Paul polishes and Quadir reads, Nicky takes a writing pad from a bedside locker.)*

**Paul:** You're an idiot, Quadir.

**Nicky:** *(as he writes on the pad)* Dear Mum and Dad, How are you? How's Jessie? How's my bedroom? How's the house? How are Jody, Ben, Ellie, Marlon and all my friends from school? How's Mr Harrington next door? How's Mr Harrington's tortoise? How's the newsagent's where I used to get sweets? How's London? I'm OK, I suppose. Love Nicky – your son in case you've forgotten. P.S. How's Beth?

**Paul:** *(sarcastically putting the shoes, now polished, on Quadir's bed)* Next time you're on your own, guy.

**Quadir:** *(looking up)* You just don't see it, do you? If you'd been born like me, you'd understand. Ever since I first heard human voices, it's been insults, humiliations. You try to ignore it, but it gets worse – they push you further and further. You have to make a stand. Once you let these people know they've got the better of you – *(He stops as Pringle returns. Pringle picks up the shoes, inspects them.)*

**Pringle:** Better.

*There's a tense pause.*

**Quadir:** You can thank Paul. He did them.

**Paul:** Gee thanks, Quadir.

**Pringle:** *(looking enraged at Paul, then at Nicky)* You are all dead meat in here.

# Speaking, Listening and Performing

In groups, read the scene. Discuss what happens and how the four boys behave, then work together to stage a performance of the scene.

You'll need to think about these issues:

● Which member of the group will play each boy? Remember that Pringle is older than the others.

● What clothes are each of the characters going to wear?

● Will you use any scenery or props? (The **props** are any items, such as chairs, that the actors need on stage.)

Remember to rehearse the scene. It's easier to move around, make gestures and put on expressions if you're not holding a book in your hand. So it's best to learn your lines!

# Developing Your Own Scripts

## Speaking and Listening

In groups, study the plot outlines on this page. Choose one of them to develop into your own short play. Develop your ideas for scenes by role-playing them, before writing the first draft of your script.

Note: a **scene** is a part of the play that is set in one place.

## The Ring

Stephen Driver hears a noise in his back garden. He sees a girl running towards him, shouting for him to let her in. As he does so, a shot is fired, which narrowly misses them.

Stephen is shocked to see that the girl is his niece, Julia. She tells him that she has been followed by two gunmen, but she doesn't know why.

Stephen notices that she is wearing a ring that once belonged to his grandmother. Julia's mother gave it to her just before she went to New Zealand, telling her never to let it out of her sight ... but she didn't tell Julia why.

Julia's great-grandmother was German. Stephen and Julia discover from reading family letters that the ring once belonged to a German prince, Count von Konisberg. It is very valuable, and an international gang of crooks want to steal it.

Stephen and Julia tell the police, and the gang are arrested. Then they fly to Germany to meet the Count's great-grandson, William Konigsberg. They give him the ring and he gives them a reward.

## Bad Company

Cheryl Watkins is devastated when her parents are killed in a boating accident. She is forced to live with an aunt she doesn't like and a cousin who hates her.

All Cheryl wanted to do was to go to drama school. But her aunt forces her to leave school and start work in a pea-canning factory.

One night at a disco she meets Kerry. She runs away from her aunt's and goes to live with Kerry and her friends. They live by shoplifting. Cheryl joins in, but is caught.

One evening, in the queue for fish and chips, she bumps into Matthew, an old school friend. He takes her for a drink and asks her out. Matthew persuades her to leave Kerry's and to apply for drama school.

The play ends when Cheryl gets a letter offering her a place at drama school.

## The Dare

Oliver never failed to try a dare. Once he dared to eat a worm. He ate the worm, and was given a bag of sweets.

Oliver never did a dare without a reward. Jacob, his friend, dared him to shout 'Toad' in Mr Phillips's class. Oliver did the dare, he was sent to the headteacher and put on an hour's detention. However, the dare cost Jacob a £1 bag of sweets and one of his baby white mice.

Soon the whole school knew about Oliver's dares. The dares got more and more difficult and dangerous.

Finally, Jacob and Marie dared Oliver to run across the busy main road outside his house. He would have won money prizes, but he ended up in hospital when he got hit by a car.

Fortunately he was not seriously hurt. From his hopital bed, Oliver promised his mum and dad and his friends that he would never play dare again. The last dare was stupid and he could have been killed.

When Oliver was back at school, with his leg in plaster, he gave a talk to his class on road safety.

Below is the first draft of the script Raheena and her group wrote for their version of *Bad Company*.

Dad: You'll be fine, Cheryl. I know your exams are coming up, but your mum and I need a break ... you know how much we like messing about on boats.

Mum: Aunt Agatha will look after you.

Cheryl: But I don't like Aunt Agatha much.

Dad: We shan't be away long

Mum: Just a week, that's all.

Cheryl: But the week turned out to be a lifetime.

Raheena and her group have begun to develop a good script. But it would be difficult for anyone to perform their play, because they have forgotten to put in any stage directions. Their script doesn't tell us:

- where the scene takes place;
- what props there are on the stage;
- how people enter or leave the stage;
- how people say certain things.

On the right is the second draft of their script with the stage directions added.

# Writing

Now draft the scripts of your play. Remember to include stage directions. You can find advice on how to lay out a script properly on page 87 of *English Direct* Book 1.

The scene opens with Cheryl and her mother sitting on a settee in the family living room. (By putting different covers over this settee and moving its position, it is also used as the settee in Aunt Agatha's living room and Kerry's flat.)

Cheryl and her mum are facing the audience. Dad walks up the stage steps, from the audience.

Dad: (pleading) You'll be fine Cheryl. I know your exams are coming up, but Mum and I need a break ... you know how much we like messing about on boats.

Mum: (turning towards Cheryl and taking hold of her hand) Aunt Agatha will look after you.

Cheryl: But I don't like Aunt Agatha much.

Dad: We shan't be away long

Mum: Just a week, that's all.

Dad takes Mum's hand. They stand up and walk off stage, down the steps and into the audience. Cheryl gets up and walks to the front of the stage. She sobs and takes a handkerchief from the pocket of her jeans.

Cheryl: (to the audience) But the week turned out to be a lifetime ...

# Putting on a Performance

When you put on a play, there are lots of different tasks that have to be done. Look at this article, which tells you about those tasks and about the people who do them.

## Who Does What in the Theatre?

**The director:** The director's job is to help the actors to plan their moves and gestures and how they speak their lines. The director takes charge of rehearsals and tells the actors which parts need practising again.

**The cast:** The cast of a play is all the actors who are taking part in it. When the director is choosing people for particular parts they think about whether the actor will be able:

★ to look like the character;
★ to act like the character;
★ to speak like the character.

**The stage manager:** This person is in charge of everything that goes on backstage. They must make sure that the actors are in position to come on at the right time. They are also in charge of making sure that the scenery is in the right position and that the stage

hands know when to move or change the furniture on stage.

**Stage hands:** This group of people are responsible for putting up the scenery and moving furniture and props between scenes. One of them will also be responsible for drawing the curtains.

**The set designer:** The set for a play is the scenery or furniture on the stage. The set designer draws sketches and plans of what the scenery will look like and where the scenery and furniture will go.

**The costume designer:** This person designs the costumes that the cast are going to wear.

**The properties manager:** This person is responsible for making a list of all the props that are needed, and for finding or making them.

**The lighting crew:**

These people are responsible for positioning and working any stage lighting that the director wants to have.

**The sound technician:** Their job is to record any music or sound effects that are needed, and to play the recordings at the right time during the performance.

# Reading

Read the article 'Who Does What in the Theatre?', then write answers to these questions.

**1** Who plans what the scenery will look like?

**2** Who moves the scenery around on the stage?

**3** Who is in charge of rehearsals?

**4** Who records any music that is needed?

**5** Who reminds the actors what to say if they forget their lines?

**6** What is the group of all the actors in a play called?

**7** What are the props?

**8** What does the stage manager do?

# Speaking and Listening

Use the resources centre to find out more about an area of play production that interests you, for example, stage lighting, sound effects, costume design or make-up. Make notes and prepare a short talk to tell the rest of the class what you have learned about it.

# Writing

- Work in a group. Design a programme for a production of the short play your group wrote. Use a word processor to draft your articles and a desk-top publishing program to produce copies of it.
- Study the information on these page, then draft an article for a teenage magazine about everything that has to be done when you're putting on a performance of a play. You can use the title 'There's more to putting on a play than acting'.

# A Class Project

Work together as a class to put on a performance of a play. You could either put on a performance of one of your short plays or choose one of the plays from the Collins playscripts series.

*The make-up team:* Their job is to make sure that any necessary make-up is available for the cast to put on.

*The programme editor:* Their job is to compile the programme and to get it printed. They will need to get a number of people to help them to design and write the programme.

*The prompter:* This person sits either in the front row of the audience or at the side of the stage. They have a copy of the script. If any of the actors forgets their lines, the prompter whispers loudly to remind them what to say.

# Accent and Dialect

Everyone speaks with an **accent**. Your accent is the way you pronounce words. When someone speaks with a strong accent, and one that you are not used to hearing, it can be difficult to understand them.

It can also be difficult to understand someone who speaks in a **regional dialect**. A **dialect** is the type of English that is spoken by a particular group of people. A regional dialect is the type of English spoken by people who live in the same area. Each dialect has its own words and expressions, as well as its own grammar.

The most widely used type of English is **Standard English**. This is the type of English that is taught in schools and used most often on the TV and radio. Because we are so used to hearing Standard English spoken, we can usually understand what other people say when they are using Standard English.

Look at the playscript 'Mixed Doubles' (right). Lee and Jamie have made a mistake, but it takes time for the misunderstanding to get sorted out because of the way the two boys speak.

*Lee* is a Geordie, who comes from the area around Newcastle-upon-Tyne in Tyne and Wear. He speaks with a strong accent and uses a regional dialect.

*Jamie* is from Scotland. He also has a strong accent and speaks in a Scottish dialect.

The two girls, *Louise and Abi,* speak Standard English. They come from Cambridge and do not have a strong accent.

## Mixed Doubles

**Scene: A tennis court at a holiday centre.**

**Lee:** Howay, yous. We haven't got till the morrer, ya knaa.

**Louise:** Pardon?

**Jamie:** Aye. Yez should be aff. It's ower the time.

**Abi:** What are they talking about?

**Louise:** I've no idea.

**Lee:** Divent look arrus like that, man. It's not us as in the wrang.

**Jamie:** We could ha' yez thrawn oot.

**Louise:** Excuse me, do you mind keeping out of the way? We're trying to finish our game.

**Abi:** Should we play a let on that last serve, Louise? I was distracted.

**Jamie:** Ach, weell, sorry for breathin'.

**Abi:** Granted,

**Jamie:** Yi cheeky deill. This is oor court.

**Abi:** Oh, really? Who are you? The All England Tennis Committee?

**Louise:** I don't think so.

**Lee:** He's not even English, he's Scotch.

**Jamie:** Scottish.

**Lee:** S'what aah said. Howay, lasses, you've gone ten minutes ower. It's wor shot noo.

**Louise:** I hope you're not going to play tennis in those boots.

**Lee:** What's a marrer wirrem? They're class, these.

**Louise:** They're for playing football.

**Lee:** They're trainin' byuts. Ye can dae owt in 'em.

**Abi:** Are they good for running?

**Lee:** Why aye.

**Abi:** Well, run over there, then. We want to finish our game.

**Jamie:** Yi dinna get it, dae yi? We've paid guid money for this. **We're** wantin' **oor** game.

**Abi:** Look … what time are you due on court?

**Lee:** Yonks ago. What d'ye think we're on aboot?

**Abi:** What time exactly?

**Jamie:** Half past.

**Louise:** Half past?

**Jamie:** (mimicking) Ooh, 'harf parst'.

**Lee:** Aye. So you've nicked nearly fifteen minutes o' wor time. Haddaway back to ya shally.

**Louise:** Actually, we've booked until four.

**Jamie:** Foor?

**Lee:** Canna be. Looka, here's wa bookin' slip. Half three till half fower. So scat.

**Abi:** Let me see that.

**Lee:** Wasa marrer? D'ye not believe us, like? Here.

**Abi:** This booking's for Court 13.

**Lee:** Aye.

**Louise:** This is Court 11.

**Lee:** Gerraway is it.

**Abi:** Read the number on the net post, dummy. What does that say?

**Jamie:** Ach, yoor jessin'!

**Lee:** So which is thurteen?

**Louise:** Over there. Where those two men have just started. Looks like you've lost your place, boys.

**Jamie:** Lee, yi neep heid!

**Lee:** Divent blame me, man. You're the one what said we had to hoi these lasses off.

**Abi:** Charming!

**Jamie:** Fit wi daein' noo? I'm nae takin' them big loons on.

**Lee:** (in his sweetest, politest voice) Er, excuse me, ladies. Would you care for a game of mixed doubles?

David Williams

# Speaking and Listening

1 In groups of four, read the script and discuss what happens in the scene. Use these questions to help you.
   ● Why do Lee and Jamie interrupt the girls' game of tennis?
   ● Why do Abi and Louise try to go on playing?
   ● What does Abi point out when Lee shows her the booking form?
   ● Why does Lee suggest a game of mixed doubles?

2 Go through the script and look at what Lee says. Notice how he sometimes uses dialect words instead of Standard English. For example, he says 'divent' instead of 'don't', and 'wor' instead of 'our'. What other dialect words and phrases does he use?
   Notice also how Lee speaks with a strong accent. He says 'ya knaa' instead of 'you know', and 'shally' instead of 'chalet'. What other examples of Lee's strong accent can you find?

3 Study what Jamie says. Notice how he too speaks in a dialect. He says 'dinna' instead of 'don't', and 'neep' instead of 'turnip'. What other Scottish words and phrases does Jamie use? Jamie also has a strong accent. Find examples of words and phrases that show how strong Jamie's accent is.

# Writing

Work as a group and produce a different version of the script in which Lee and Jamie speak Standard English and do not have strong accents. Here is the start of such a script.

**Lee:** Off you go. We haven't got until tomorrow, you know.

**Louise:** Pardon?

**Jamie:** Yes. You should be off. It's over the time.

# Glossary and Index

**Accent** Your accent is the way you pronounce words. *See pages 94–95.*

**Adjective** An adjective is a word that tells you more about a noun, for example, 'delicious' or 'red'. *See page 34.*

**Adverb** An adverb is a word that adds information about part of the sentence, usually the verb. 'Slowly', 'now' and 'here' are all adverbs. *See page 85.*

**Apostrophe** The apostrophe is shaped like a comma. It is used in two ways: to show where a letter or letters have been missed out of a word (as in 'don't'), and to show that something belongs to someone (as in 'Mum's car'). *See pages 76–77.*

**Comma** A comma is a punctuation mark used to break up lists of words and to separate the different parts of long sentences. *See pages 68–69.*

**Comparison poem** A comparison poem is a poem in which comparisons are made. Colour poems, opposites poems and simile poems are all comparison poems. *See pages 42–49.*

**Conjunction** A conjunction is a word that joins words or sentences. 'And', 'but', 'because' and 'if' are all conjunctions. *See page 65.*

**Dialect** A dialect is a type of English that is spoken by a particular group of people. *See pages 94–95.*

**DTP** DTP is an abbreviation for 'desk-top publishing'. A DTP program can be used to design and produce magazines and other material on a computer. *See page 58.*

**Latin** Latin was the language used by the Romans and in much of medieval Europe. *See pages 80–81.*

**Middle English** Middle English was the form of the English language used in the Middle Ages. *See pages 80–81.*

**Moral** The moral of a story is the message that the story gives to the reader. *See page 84.*

**Noun** A noun is any word that is the name of a thing, a person, a feeling or an idea. *See page 34.*

**Old English** Old English, or Anglo-Saxon, was the form of the English language used from Saxon times to about 1100. *See pages 80–81.*

**Old Norse** Old Norse was the language used by the Vikings. *See pages 80–81.*

**Paragraph** A paragraph is a group of sentences, all of which are about the same idea or subject. *See page 11.*

**Phrase** A phrase is a group of words that only makes full sense as part of a sentence. *See page 68.*

**Plot** The plot of a story is the outline of the series of events that happen in the story. *See page 84.*

**Prop** The props are any objects, such as chairs, that the actors need on stage. *See page 89.*

**Regional dialect** A regional dialect is the type of English spoken by people who live in the same area. *See pages 94–95.*

**Scene** The scene is a part of the play that is set in one place. *See page 90.*

**Simile** A simile is a statement that compares one thing to another. 'He trembled like a leaf' is a simile. *See pages 44–45.*

**Slogan** A slogan is a word or phrase used by advertisers to persuade you to do things or buy things. *See page 32.*

**Standard English** Standard English is a common dialect of English, the one used by news presenters and taught in schools. *See page 94.*

**Tense** The tense of a verb tells you whether an action is taking place in the present, in the past or in the future. *See page 13.*

**Typeface** A typeface is the style in which text can be printed. *See page 58.*

**Verb** A verb is an action word – a word that tells us what people or things are doing or being. *See page 13.*

**Voice-over** A voice-over is an off-screen voice on television, film or radio that tells or comments on the story. *See page 39.*